THE NEW WORLD AND THE NEW WORLD ORDER

The New World and the New World Order

US Relative Decline, Domestic Instability in the Americas and the End of the Cold War

K. R. Dark
Department of Politics
University of Reading
and
Clare Hall
University of Cambridge

with

A. L. Harris
Department of Politics
University of Reading

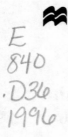

First published in Great Britain 1996 by
MACMILLAN PRESS LTD
Houndmills, Basingstoke, Hampshire RG21 6XS
and London
Companies and representatives
throughout the world

A catalogue record for this book is available
from the British Library.

ISBN 0–333–64804–8

First published in the United States of America 1996 by
ST. MARTIN'S PRESS, INC.,
Scholarly and Reference Division,
175 Fifth Avenue,
New York, N.Y. 10010

ISBN 0–312–16212–X

Library of Congress Cataloging-in-Publication Data
Dark, K. R. (Ken R.)
The New World and the new world order : U. S. relative decline,
domestic instability in the Americas and the end of the Cold War /
K. R. Dark, A. L. Harris.
p. cm.
Includes bibliographical references and index.
ISBN 0–312–16212–X (cloth)
1. United States—Foreign relations—1989– 2. United States–
–Politics and government—1989– 3. Canada—Politics and
government—1980– 4. America—Politics and government—20th
century. 5. Imperialism—History—20th century. 6. World
politics—1985–1995. 7. Cold War. I. Harris, A. L. II. Title.
E840.D36 1996
327.73—dc20
                                                    96–32096
                                                    CIP

10   9   8   7   6   5   4   3   2   1
05   04   03   02   01   00   99   98   97   96

Printed and bound in Great Britain by
Antony Rowe Ltd, Chippenham, Wiltshire

Contents

Preface

This book aims to examine several inter-related issues: these centre on the 'decline' debate about the USA and the question of its post-Cold War role, but include other debates about the historical significance of the Cold War and the character of the USA as a political unit.

In reviewing these (much discussed) questions, the approach taken here is somewhat different from that of previous studies, in that not only is it based on the international history or international political economy of the USA and the twentieth-century international system, but it also attempts to combine them with a long-term comparative historical approach which examines the domestic affairs of the Americas as a whole, rather than the foreign affairs and economic context of the USA alone. As such, far greater attention is given to the polities both to the South and North of the USA, and especially to the changes taking place within America, than has been accorded to these matters by other analysts of these questions.

Likewise, the approach here is different from those so far used in the 'decline debate', in that it introduces cultural factors into the discussion and places them, rather than economics, at the centre of this study. Another difference lies in the way in which political, social, cultural and economic trends derived from contemporary and historical data are analysed: the approach here offers a new suggestion for the resolution of a long-standing problem limiting the utility of 'trend-projection' as a basis for evaluating global change.

To do so, this work draws on approaches developed elsewhere in the study of the dynamics of complex systems and integrates these with perspectives from social science. Consequently, this book contains both an empirical component and a theoretical element, which might hopefully be of use to scholars working on other questions. Whereas the remainder of the book was written afresh, Chapter 3 is mostly a revised version of A. L. Harris's unpublished 1993 University of Nottingham BA dissertation supervised by A. M. Timpson.

Finally, it remains only to thank our families for their continuing support and help, Tim Farmiloe and Annabelle Buckley at Macmillan for their assistance in publishing this study and Professor Christoph Bluth of the University of Reading for agreeing to include it in this series. Our thanks also to many colleagues who have discussed aspects of this work with us, and offered their encouragement. Any failings or mistakes, however, remain our own.

K. R. Dark
A. L. Harris
March 1996

1 The Fall of the American Empire?

In order to attempt to understand the current international politics of the USA, and its future prospects, in relation to four themes – the questions of 'relative decline', the character of the USA itself as a modern state, the meaning (in historical terms) of the Cold War and its end, and the significance of the 'New World Order' – the approach used here is both historical and theoretical. It is historical in that it relies on an empirical historical understanding for its basis, and theoretical both in that it seeks to refine the technique of 'trend analysis' in order to address the more prospective questions raised by these issues, and in attempting to redress the current tendency to over-emphasise economic and military factors as opposed to the role of culture in international affairs.

These questions are of interest primarily because of the importance attached by both policy-makers and other scholars to the prospects of the USA in the post-Cold War world, and in particular to the question of whether the USA is 'in decline'. This study employs two new perspectives on this issue. First, this question is viewed in domestic terms, and in social, cultural, ideological and religious terms, rather than in terms of global strategy and economics alone. Second, the USA is seen as closely related to continent-wide processes of change in the Americas – the 'New World' of our title – as well as to world affairs in a broader sense. Our study is, therefore, of 'America'[1] in the Americas, and in international politics.

The reconsideration of the character of the USA itself is essentially a historical question: what is the modern USA? The answer given here is that it is a continental empire, formed by colonisation, settlement, conquest and acculturation. This interpretation must not be seen as entirely negative, however, since a different definition of imperialism is used here from that usually employed by scholars of political science and international history.

The second of these new approaches is primarily theoretical: by emphasising the concept of 'initial states' (the structuring role of origins), drawn from the mathematics of complexity, and the constraining role of cultural development, it is possible to show that new emphasis may be placed on the process of state-formation itself, and on the early development of the state, in understanding its later political development.[2] This, it is argued, permits the definition of primary and enduring characteristics which continue to play a fundamental role in politics and society. Using such characteristics, an answer is suggested to the key problem limiting the utility of trend analysis: how can one decide which trends will persist and which will fade out?

Consequently, this book contains both empirically- and theoretically-based approaches and links the study of early American history to that of modern America. It provides a logical attempt to evaluate which characteristics of the contemporary USA will be significant to its development in the twenty-first century.

The structure of the book follows this framework, with Chapter 1 redefining the USA in a comparative historical context and considering arguments, on general grounds, that it is in decline. This addresses issues of international politics and approaches to large-scale political change.

Chapter 2 examines the processes of decline and internal disarray which are identifiable within the USA and Canada. It is argued that these form part of the same pattern of continent-wide processes of change. The following chapter is a detailed examination of the country in which these processes of fragmentation have reached their most acute phase so far: Canada, and in particular, Quebec. It is argued that the Canadian experience of separatism may lead both to major geopolitical changes and 'knock-on' effects in the USA itself. Rather than being a unique aspect of national political development, the Quebec case illustrates more general trends towards regional separatism and cultural fragmentation.

Chapter 4 addresses the question of the relationship between state-formation and contemporary politics, and the 'calibration' of trend analysis, using the theory of 'initial states'. Last, an attempt is made, albeit tentatively, to set out an alternative model for the future of the USA in international politics and of the domestic character of America in the twenty-first century.

THE FALL OF THE AMERICAN EMPIRE?

Chapter 1 aims to demonstrate that the twentieth century view of the USA as a 'nation-state' is incorrect and that America is more accurately seen as an empire. Such a claim may, to some, recall Cold War propaganda and 'New Left' critiques of the USA, but it is made on fundamentally different grounds.[3] Both of those perspectives on US politics saw imperialism in the context of American foreign policy and US economic interests abroad, and viewed it as intrinsically evil. While doubtless there are imperialist characteristics discernible in both of these facets of US affairs, it is not on these grounds that the contemporary USA is defined as an empire in this work. Instead, it is the internal process of colonisation, cultural domination and the retention of regions seized by military conquest in North America itself which demonstrates the imperial character of the USA.

While not unaware of the potential critiques of this position which may be made by scholars appalled at the concept of a US empire,[4] these depend upon how one defines imperialism. So, it must be pointed out at the outset that, while neither advocating imperialism nor defending its historical legacy, imperialism cannot be seen as a wholly negative experience for the peoples involved (both of what world-systems analysts might call the 'core' and 'periphery'). Nor is this book a product of anti-Americanism or of a Marxist agenda; it is written (in part) in reply to Paul Kennedy's work[5] and as a contribution both to the debate which he began and to the ongoing debates on the end of the Cold War, America's new international role and the relationship between domestic and international politics. It is also intended as a contribution to the theory of analysing long-term trends in international affairs, and that of employing historical data and the analysis of cultural factors in political science.

This being the case, it will be clear that the aim of this work is to provide a balanced account of the contemporary history and the domestic and international politics of the USA. In so far as this book has a political purpose in the present at all, this is – at least in part – to alert scholars and others to the potential risk of domestic crisis in both the USA and Canada, and the serious implications which this would have for international relations in general.

Consequently, it is hoped that both US citizens and non-Americans will find the argument here both persuasive and interesting. It carries with it wide-ranging implications for the international and domestic politics of the Americas (not just the USA) and addresses issues which have been at the heart of recent US governmental and business concerns. These include questions of US 'relative decline', the post-Cold War international order, the role of the USA in world politics and the relationship between domestic and international politics.

For clarity of argument, this chapter will begin by considering some studies of the nature of imperialism which have been carried out by other scholars. Then, the question of how these relate to US foreign policy and international economic affairs, the usual subject of discussions of 'American imperialism', will be addressed. A new definition of imperialism is proposed, which will then be used to examine these aspects of US politics. This will lead into a discussion of the relationship between US international politics and domestic affairs, and finally to an examination of the question, following the end of the Cold War, of whether or not the USA is in decline.

PAST WORK ON IMPERIALISM

Although O'Connor could identify three doctrines of imperialism, of which one saw it as dissociated from capitalism, since the time of Hobson's classic *Imperialism: a study*, political scientists have tended to see imperialism in a perspective dominated by the two characteristics of modernity and capitalism.[6] The perception that imperialism is a product of capitalism involves the characterisation of imperialism in economic terms, a view developed by Lenin and Hilferding within a Marxist context.[7] A similarly economistic approach has been taken by opponents of these scholars, such as Schumpeter, leading to the use of political economy and economic theory as the basis of both definitions of, and explanations for, imperialism.[8] For Schumpeter, imperialism was defined by aimless and unlimited expansion, resulting from a combination of psychological, military and economic factors. Interestingly, in contrast to Lenin, Schumpeter considered imperialism to be inimical to capitalism and the combination of capitalism and liberal democracy to be the force which would bring an end to imperialism. As such, Schumpeter's model of imperialism was – from start to finish – grounded in the political effects of economic factors, alongside other non-material aspects.

This is not to say that all theorists of imperialism have opted for an economic definition. As Galtung pointed out, it is not necessary to use economics as the central defining feature of imperialism, although the examples he uses (Schumpeter and Hobson) in fact did; neither has its explanation always been seen in economic terms.[9] There have been scholars who have used both a political definition and a political explanation for imperialism. For example, Foeken and Mansergh used political rather than economic factors to define and explain imperialism, while Thornton saw an empire in more general terms: as the 'effective control' of an 'external system'.[10]

Other scholars have adopted an approach based on the mutual interests of elites, combining political critique and political explanation. In particular, one may highlight the work of Robinson, who saw empires as arising from the shared interests of elites rather than economic factors themselves.[11] The second general characteristic of earlier work on imperialism has been to characterise it solely with reference to the fifteenth- to twentieth-century European empires (such as those of Britain, Spain, France, Portugal and Tsarist Russia). Again, there are exceptions to this general rule – Lichtheim's discussion, for instance, encompassed both the Ancient and Modern worlds[12] – but this has been the predominant trend in recent accounts of this subject.

The current discussion of theories of imperialism in international relations has remained, however, principally tied to the notions of political economic definitions and explanations, alongside a focus on the modern world empires. An excellent example of this is Galtung's well-known paper on the structural theory of imperialism.[13] This adopts a core:periphery framework for analysis and develops the view of a commonalty of interest between the elites of the core and those of the periphery. This view has been developed by other scholars, enriching the debate with new theoretical perspectives, such as Taylor's 'world systems' reformulation of the political geography of imperialism, and Buchanan's discussion of US economic dominance in the post-World War II world as 'the new shape of empire'.[14] Other scholars have been less tolerant of the view that imperialism may survive in post-World War II international politics. For example, O'Brien argued that the Soviet Union did not have an empire,[15] although since the collapse of communism other scholars have felt at more liberty to talk about the former USSR as if it was undoubtedly a formal empire.

DEFINING 'IMPERIALISM'

Before one can discuss whether or not any state is 'imperial' the question of how one defines an 'empire' must be raised. There are many possible alternatives.[16] For example, one might say that an empire is a state which has grown larger through the conquest of its neighbours: but that would exclude those empires which have formed through a mixture of conquest and treaty, such as the Roman empire.

One might take an economic view, and say that an empire is a state which unfairly exploits other territories which it controls but does not include within its own territorial boundaries. This would, however, exclude the French approach to imperialism in the post-World War II period in which areas of the French empire were classified as parts of metropolitan France.[17] An alternative approach would be to emphasise the aspect of economic exploitation, and see empires as territories in which the core state economically exploits and commercially dominates the colonial states of the periphery – but this would again be to exclude those empires, such as the British empire, in which core states entered into two-way trade with the periphery.[18] Last, there is of course the classic Marxist definition of imperialism in economic terms: the empire as the 'highest' form of capitalism.[19] If this is so, however, why were there so many pre-capitalist (in Marxist terms) states which developed into pre-industrial empires? A notable example is the Roman empire, the collapse of which is said to indicate the origins of European feudalism, according to Marxist historians. Consequently, there may be problems with all of these views of imperialism which stress the economic character of imperial systems. If economics alone does not permit an easy definition of imperialism, perhaps this can be found in political terms? In order to define an empire in a way which can be used in the study of contemporary international relations, it seems preferable to ask what those states, which we habitually accept as undoubted 'empires' in world history, share in common.

Looking at the cases of the British, Spanish, French, Portuguese, German and Russian empires in the modern world, some common characteristics can be discerned.[20] In each case they were formed throughout the expansion of the core state by a mixture of conquest and treaty. In each case they formed through the inclusion of previously sovereign territories, although not necessarily other states, into a single system dominated by the core state. All had an economic system which presented the core state and its citizens with economic opportunities and advantages *vis-à-vis* the inhabitants of the peripheral or colonial territories. All used force to control peripheral populations and all had, to some extent, a negative impact on at least parts of those peripheral populations, whether by design (for example, genocide) or accident (such as by spreading disease). All of these empires also showed evidence of the acculturation of minorities within their territories, although none of them were culturally homogenous.

It is especially important here to note that the impacts on peripheral populations, in every case, also involved both material and other benefits (for example, intellectual/spiritual benefits), as these were perceived by contemporaries among the peripheral populations and by later historians. The spread of Western medicine and its effects on health and mortality rates is a clear example of both of these aspects in the twentieth century.

Consequently, one cannot say that any of these empires were entirely negative experiences for the peripheral populations, although neither were they entirely positive experiences for those populations. Another important factor is that in each case the imperial core state legitimised its actions by reference to activities such as 'civilising' the periphery or bringing enhanced cultural values or economic developments. So, in these terms, a 'check list' of imperial characteristics can be built up from which we can recognise whether or not a state is an empire.

To give a practical example, most scholars would agree that the Roman empire under Hadrian was an empire.[21] It was certainly formed through a mixture of conquest and treaty, and had a culturally heterogeneous population. Acculturation to Roman norms occurred in the periphery and among minorities in Rome itself. The state ideology emphasised Roman cultural and intellectual superiority and saw the role of the empire as 'civilising' the 'barbarians' of the periphery. Within the empire an advantage was obtained for traders from the core areas over the peripheral populations. Violence was used against such populations, although they definitely received material (and perceived intellectual) benefits from the experience of empire. The peripheral populations were also held under a harsh imperial system which gave no opportunity for self-determination and was prepared to act against those local cultural and religious groups it perceived as a threat to the state. This example would therefore be classified as an empire by the definition suggested on (other) historical grounds.

To consider a state which most scholars would probably agree was not an empire, take the example of modern Fiji. It does not include territories outside of the core state, and the other characteristics are accordingly lacking. Consequently, this list of attributes may be used as a working definition of an empire.

The contemporary US administration would assiduously stress that the US is not, and never has been, an empire. To some scholars, such as Liska and Aaron,[22] this claim is refuted by US foreign policy; the work of Williams has already been mentioned. Other scholars have argued that the USA exhibits 'informal imperialism' (the term was first coined in this context by Gallagher and Robinson);[23] the role that the USA has played in the process of decolonisation in the twentieth century tends to support the official US view that its foreign policy has not been 'imperialistic'. It has strongly supported human rights and, most of all, the principle of self-determination. It might, there-fore, be supposed that the American claim to be free from the taint of imperialism is well-founded, countering critics (mainly of the Marxist left and writing during the Cold War) who have cited the existence of widespread economic influence as evidence of US imperialism.[24] There seems, however, no reason to claim that such economic links alone make the USA an empire, given the extent of internationalisation vis-ible in the contemporary world economy. Likewise, the Soviet usage of 'Imperialist' to describe the West, and the USA in particular, was propagandist in character.[25]

While the economic argument may have less strength than often supposed, the argument that American support for national self-deter-mination is incompatible with the view that the USA is imperialist is unfounded. In its Balkan policy in the nineteenth century the UK con-sistently supported a policy of self-determination for the peoples of the former Ottoman empire. This was at the height of British imperi-alism itself, and refutes the view that self-determination is a key piece of evidence for a non-imperial state.

The issue of detecting imperialism in US foreign affairs has been much-debated, as pointed out earlier, by the New Left in the 1980s, which saw US foreign policy as little more than the intervention of the USA in world affairs; but it might be argued that the concept of informal imperialism is convenient when America's international role in the post-Cold War world is examined.

Such a discussion brings us to the relationship between the defini-tion of imperialism formulated above and the case of the USA. This state was formed by the European conquest of part of a non-European continent, an imperialistic legacy, as Williams argued.[26] The use of violence in this conquest is well known, as are both its positive and negative effects on the native American population.

AMERICAN FOREIGN AFFAIRS AND US IMPERIALISM[27]

The role of treaties in forming the American state is slightly less well-known to non-Americanists, but one recalls for instance the annexa-tion of Texas (1845) as a clear example of this, or – for another example – the acquisition of Alaska (1867). Interestingly, conquest rather than treaty was not simply a mode of US state-formation reserved for inter-action with 'non-Europeans'. Much of what is today the South West USA, including San Francisco harbour itself, became part of the USA as a result of the Treaty of Guadeloupe (1848) which ended war with Mexico, and the subsequent 'Mexican Cession'. The following decade was to see the election of Franklin Pierce, whose 'Young America' policy was designed to prompt territorial expansion. In these new territories the economic advantage of US citizens over local populations was overwhelming.

These actions were legitimised by the claim that in expanding the USA in this way, the Americans were 'civilising' the continent and promoting economic growth. Although these characteristics demonstrate that the USA has an 'imperial past', in the terms in which imperialism has been defined in this chapter, they do not relate directly to modern America.

While such trends may easily be traced to the end of the nineteenth century, evidence for their persistence into the twentieth century is more controversial. Schwabe argued that soon after the US victory over Spain in 1898 (which resulted in the annexation of the Philippines, Cuba and Puerto Rico), Theodore Roosevelt and the Republican party 'increasingly came to have misgivings', and that 'the conditions which bred the imperialist atmosphere of 1898 no longer existed'. Yet even Schwabe acknowledges that the subsequent 'Roosevelt Corollary' of 1905 to the 'Monroe doctrine' (effectively giving the USA a role as an 'international policeman' in Latin America) extends this pattern into the early years of the twentieth century.[28] Although this was itself declared invalid soon after its proclamation, Schwabe's claim that 'The administrations after Wilson never returned to a policy of traditional imperialism' is highly debatable.[29] The next part of the quotation, from the perspective of the 1990s, puts his interpretation into a clearer context:

> Since 1913 the American government's conception of its national role and stated intention of its foreign policies have been as non-imperialistic as those of the Soviet government since the October Revolution.[30]

The end of the Cold War has brought with it the near-universal acknowledgement among political scientists of the imperialistic character of the former Soviet Union. Might this not also prompt a reconsideration of the same question with reference to the United States, and why should empires have to state openly their imperialistic tendencies in order to be perceived as empires?

Continuing the historical narrative, albeit in outline, serves to demonstrate a degree of continuity between US imperialism in the nineteenth century and current US policies both at home and abroad. For example, the US interventions in Haiti in 1913 and the acquisition of the Danish Virgin Islands in 1915 both occurred after the election of Woodrow Wilson and after Schwabe's alleged end of American formal imperialism.

This was not the only foreign intervention during Wilson's presidency which attempted to secure US policies against local self-determination, as witnessed by the subsequent action in Mexico. As the Mexican intervention was coming to an end, Wilson brought the USA into World War I and, immediately following that, into Russia in 1918. Again, the aim was to secure US policies in relation to the Russian state.

It might be argued that Wilson did all of this for altruistic motives and because of his idealistic world view. This is probably correct, but does not alter the character of the actions themselves: one does not assess whether Roman or British imperialism was 'imperialistic' simply by evaluating the degree of altruism involved in political decisions. Plainly, as a form of foreign policy and a type of international action, imperialism can be used to further completely laudable aims, although obviously it is often used for less high-minded reasons. Wilson was attempting to impose an American order on the world, whether other nations wanted this or not.

A clear continuity can be seen in US imperialism until the end of World War I, a pattern consolidated in the role of the USA in the inter-War years. There is, however, little doubt that the inter-War years saw the USA pursuing a policy of relative isolationism, and while this too may find an analogy in the 'Little Britain' policy of nineteenth-century British imperialists, the next overseas assertion of the USA came in its participation in World War II.

Although US policy originally favoured a view which would see the emergence of regional 'spheres of influence' in the post-War world and in which each victorious 'great power' would act again as a 'policeman', this was given up in favour of stressing global unity. The re-formulation of this policy to shift from regionalism to 'globalism', shows the continued existence of a trend in US foreign policy-making, which asserted a wider role for the USA. The willingness of the US government to 'project' national 'power' on a global scale in the ensuing Cold War is, of course, well-known. The Korea, Vietnam, Granada and Haiti interventions in the 1950s, '60s, '70s, '80s and '90s all demonstrate a continuity of US willingness to use military intervention. This has not been simply in support of threatened allies, but to further US views on the 'correct' form of domestic political and economic organisation in other states.

The end of the Cold War has reduced the potential military and diplomatic costs of such overseas action. Again, in its attempt to enforce a 'New World Order', the USA has been willing to intervene in the domestic affairs of sovereign states, at least as overtly as did the Soviet Union. The problem of whether this has been for admirable reasons, or not, is unimportant in considering the question of whether this represents a continuation of US imperialism from the nineteenth century until the present.

Even from this brief summary, a continuous trend of overseas military intervention can be demonstrated, which has consistently aimed at imposing an 'American' order on the world. Since at least the end of the nineteenth century this order has been viewed in an idealistic fashion by US policy-makers, who have consistently used the language of 'world policing' and the support of liberty and democracy. In this century this has also been combined with the establishment of global institutions aimed at ensuring collective action (the League of Nations and the United Nations) in the face of threats to this idealistic model of international affairs. The most recent formulation of this viewpoint is called the 'New World Order' and its principal institutional foundation is the United Nations, but this is no more than a continuation of a long-lasting theme in US foreign policy.

Consequently, one can see that the international history of the USA shows evidence that American imperialism is a current aspect of international affairs. That this need not be interpreted as a denunciation or condemnation of the USA is also evidenced by the observation that it has been an attempt to impose 'US' values of liberty and democracy on the world. These values are, of course, subscribed to by others among the Western Allies. They are also those which many readers might personally favour as political concepts. This serves to stress that to classify a state as 'imperialistic' need not be to make an immediate condemnation of every aspect of its policy, or of its motivations for imperialism.

Such a consideration merely addresses the issue of whether US foreign policy and international actions provide evidence of continuing imperialism. A key thesis in relation to this book is that US domestic affairs can also be seen according to the same model. In order to demonstrate that this imperialistic trend is detectable in domestic as well as international politics, the next section of this chapter will attempt to tie together both patterns of imperialism, those relating to external and internal expansion and domination. To do so, it will obviously be necessary to repeat some information already outlined in the previous section, but only where this is essential to the overall argument, and in the course of this analysis these incidents will be discussed in more detail, so as to illustrate the points in question. In order to consider this more detailed evidence in a structured way, it will be divided into sections examining US territorial imperialism, economic imperialism, imperialism in foreign policy and, finally, 'cultural imperialism'. These topics have been studied by most scholars in relation to the issue of US imperialism in general and all are, of course, interconnected. So, the division made here is primarily one of analytical convenience rather than being implicit in American politics.

TERRITORIAL IMPERIALISM[31]

The 1787 Constitution of the United States was signed by the representatives of the 13 colonies by June 1790, and was enshrined as law in an area stretching from New Hampshire in the north to Georgia in the south, and which did not extend westwards beyond West Virginia or North Carolina. This is a small part of the territory which the USA claims as its own today.

Even at its foundation the expansionist forces were present in the USA. In 1776 the signatories to the Declaration of Independence put pressure on the colonists to the north, in what is now Canada, to join in the rebellion against the British. In the UK, as early as 1774, the government was already sufficiently concerned that the 13 colonies might succeed in winning over the north to a more independent approach that it had passed the Quebec Act. This Act allowed the francophone *canadiens* to retain their language, their Roman Catholicism, and their French legal system, so encouraging greater loyalty to the Crown. While this may have been a dangerous precedent to set in a multicultural empire, it did, however, fulfil its objective: to act as a disincentive to the *canadiens* to join the rebelling colonists to the south after the outbreak of the American Revolution.

By 1836 the geographical area of the USA had been vastly extended beyond its 1783 borders. It now included the whole of the Mississippi basin to the west, Florida to the south, and Maine to the north. The 'Louisiana Purchase', a huge tract of land, (in)famously bought from Napoleon for a mere 15 million dollars in 1803, had more than doubled the area of the USA when Jefferson concluded the treaty with the French, despite the dubious legality of the deal: purchase of territory was not mentioned in the Constitution. The large area under the governance of the USA might well have been even bigger had American attempts to invade British North America not been thwarted by the British in the War of 1812. In the first decade of the nineteenth century the desire for land induced the US government to 'persuade' many 'Indian' tribes to sign away their land. By 1811 a strong Shawnee leader, Tecumseh, had emerged. His determination to form an Indian confederation worried the Governor of Indiana Territory, whose forces defeated the Shawnee tribe at the Battle of Tippecanoe in November of that year. The conviction that the British were behind the 'Indian' unrest, both on the northern American border and on the border with Spain in the south-east, spread through the House of Representatives. One member of the House reported, 'We have heard but one word – like the whip-poor-will, but one eternal monotonous tone – Canada! Canada! Canada!'.[32] Jefferson himself described the annexation of the Canadas as 'a mere matter of marching'.[33] Nevertheless, despite this enthusiasm for conquest, and the preoccupation of the British with the war in Europe against Napoleon, the colonists north of the USA refused to capitulate to American pressures.

Only a few years after the pre-1836 expansion, the USA had absorbed yet more territory by force, this time taking the northern part of newly independent Mexico in the 1846–48 Mexican War. During the 1840s, too, the USA obtained the Oregon and Washington Territories from the British. In 1867 Andrew Jackson's Secretary of State, William Seward, negotiated to buy Alaska from the Russians for 7.2 million dollars. Seward was anxious to prevent it falling into the hands of the British, and also hoped that it would help persuade the British Columbians that annexation by the USA would be preferable to joining the newly formed Canadian Confederation. In 1866, and again in 1870, Irish–American bands, the Fenians, made border attacks on British North America. Their aim was to use the Canadas to provoke war between the UK and the USA, in the hope that this would win Irish independence. These were no more than minor incursions and ultimately unsuccessful; for our purposes their significance lies in the level of sympathy they received from the American people, and the implicit support of the US government for these actions.[34]

The annexation of Hawaii was a less peaceful process than the acquisition of Alaska. The USA bought most of its sugar from the Hawaiian islands; in 1875 Hawaii and the USA signed a reciprocal trade agreement which disallowed duty on Hawaiian sugar. By the end of the nineteenth century, however, the USA's increasing awareness of affairs in the Pacific region, and 'Pacific identity' prompted it to amend the trade agreement. A provision was inserted for the USA to maintain a naval base at Pearl Harbour. By 1887 the numbers of Americans settling in Hawaii had increased so rapidly that the USA had the political ability to alter the structure of the Hawaiian government. The King was forced to relinquish control and to call for the formation of a constitutional and democratic government, which came to be dominated by the American settlers. Six years later, a treaty of annexation failed to be ratified in the Senate after an investigation by incoming President, Grover Cleveland, reported 'that Americans on the islands had acted improperly . . . [and] most Hawaiians opposed annexation'.[35] Nevertheless, the American dominated government of Hawaii refused Cleveland's proposal that the monarchy should regain some of its position. It proclaimed Hawaii to be a republic in 1894, and drew up a Constitution which provided for formal annexation at a later date.

The urge for 'Westward Expansion' preoccupied the USA while the European powers were themselves engaged in empire-building. Even by the 1890s, when the 'Scramble for Africa' was taking place, the USA was consolidating and organising its territory in the west of the North American continent. By the end of the decade, the USA was increasingly aware of the Pacific region lying beyond its western borders. Like the British and the Portuguese, the Americans were interested in the future of the Far East, seeing it as a source of trade and wealth. They had already been instrumental in the opening up of Japan to the Western world, through the American Commodore Matthew Perry who had initiated diplomatic and commercial links with that country. In China, the USA invested both traders and soldiers, expecting to reap rich dividends in an American–Chinese relationship. In 1900 the USA sent soldiers to help suppress the Boxer Rebellion, and shortly afterwards President McKinley's Secretary of State, John Hay, proclaimed the famous 'Open Door' policy. This statement made it known that the USA did not want 'China's territorial and administrative entity' to be disrupted by outside governments.[36] The USA intended to stop a single European power from taking China for itself and, indeed, succeeded because the European powers felt too weak to attempt such an action. In this respect, it acted as if it were itself a nineteenth-century European 'great power'.

The heeding of the 'Open Door' policy suggested to the USA that the European powers, and the British in particular, were in decline. The British attempted no other territorial gain in China after the acquisition of Hong Kong in 1897, and began simultaneously to withdraw the Royal Navy from the Caribbean.

The USA was, therefore, forced to face the prospect of taking responsibility for the protection of its overseas interests, although an actual overseas invasion of the USA at the beginning of the twentieth century was extremely unlikely. This coincided with the rapid industrialisation of the USA, and the associated growth of large cities such as Philadelphia, Chicago and New York. Immigrants, many of whom had come to the USA to escape the effects of overpopulation in the 'Old World', were disturbed to observe such rapid urbanisation and industrialisation. There was a widespread fear that the American markets would not be able to cope with the new demands on production made by the rapid population growth. The destabilising effect of these trends was most poignantly captured by the Modernist school of American literature. Writers such as Theodore Drieser and Stephen Crane invented characters in emotional turmoil, lonely and 'depersonified' in the large city, which was often represented as a battlefield.

In this period the USA again looked outside its borders for relief from its domestic problems. Its victory in the Spanish–American War of 1898 (itself arguably an indirect consequence of the rivalry between newspaper publishers William Randolph Hearst and Joseph Pulitzer) ensured US political and economic influence over, if not control of, a vast area of Latin America. Puerto Rico, Guam and the Philippines were claimed as US territory. Spain was driven out of Latin America by the USA, in July 1898, following the Battle of Santiago Bay. The emerging independence movement in the Philippines was quashed by the Americans, but not before a three-year struggle had demonstrated its popular and enduring support. In the USA, McKinley was re-elected to the Presidency, easily beating the Democrat, William Bryan, who ran on an anti-imperialist platform. Until their independence in July 1946, the Philippines were fiercely defended as vital to US security; their proximity to Japan made it imperative that Japanese expansionism should be guarded against.

Pressures from the business world prompted the USA to retain its influence in Latin America, and to seek both new markets for American goods and unprocessed goods for the American factories and domestic markets. In 1889 the Pan-American Union was set up; this legitimised US intervention in Latin America. It was a US-dominated organisation with its headquarters located in Washington DC, and the US Secretary of State was the permanent chairman. The Union proved to be a useful vehicle for the USA after 1914 when the British withdrew many of their business interests from South America.

In the early years of the twentieth century, however, Cuba, an American protectorate after the Spanish–American War, was more important to the American economy than states in South America. Cuba was a valuable source of raw materials. This is reflected in its 1901 Constitution. The Platt Amendment to the Constitution stated that the US government could intervene in the affairs of Cuba to 'maintain government adequate for the protection of life, property and individual liberty'.[37] The arrangement with Cuba was so useful for American businesses that the island rapidly became a popular destination for Americans wanting to travel outside the USA, usually for the first time. In 1903, in Columbia, the USA engineered a revolt, the yield of which was another new, American-controlled state: Panama. American businesses then sought, and were given, permission to build a canal across Panama, to which the US government was given direct access.

It might be argued that territorial imperialism can only exist if there is a political agenda or programme driving it. It is, therefore, relevant to ask whether any such programme is discernible in US political culture.

In 1845 newspaper editor John Louis O'Sullivan coined the term 'manifest destiny' to describe the expansion of the US territory towards the Pacific coast.[38] This term was widely used to justify the forcible taking of thousands of acres of 'Indian' homelands, and much of northern Mexico. In the early 1830s Secretary of State William Seward applied the idea to US action outside mainland USA. He proclaimed that the USA must dominate 'on the Pacific ocean, and its islands and continents'.[39] Later in the nineteenth century, the Social Darwinist, John Fiske, wrote that the 'Anglo-Saxon race' was destined to rule the social, political and economic fabric of the globe.[40] It is interesting to question the extent to which the USA has continued to maintain, or reject, the use of the term 'Manifest Destiny' and the attitudes which accompanied it. If it applied only to territorial expansion on the North American continent, then, perhaps, it is a redundant term in modern American politics.

This redundancy, it might be argued, is because there are few such 'unclaimed' territories left in the continental Americas. If, however, 'Manifest Destiny' can be applied to economic, political and cultural expansion, then the USA might be said to have consistently exercised imperialism employing this ideology. But, if it is at most ambiguous, and probably doubtful, whether such an attitude underlies contemporary US relations with neighbouring lands, it certainly played a key role during the phase of territorial expansion which established the mainland territory of the contemporary USA.

So, despite the numerous analyses heralding 'American decline', which have appeared at times throughout Henry Luce's so-called 'American

Century', the USA has remained an important regional and global actor, a regional hegemon, but it has also pursued an imperialistic policy both inside and outside of the Americas. Even if its political and economic 'power' relative to some European and Asia–Pacific Rim states has declined in the 1970s and 1980s, it was still such when the Cold War ended. In 1981 the USA accounted for 20 per cent of global production, and 50 per cent of the world's exports (in US dollars).[41] Although by 1985 the USA was a debtor, rather than a creditor, nation, it was still able to borrow against its own currency, because the dollar was the medium of economic exchange for 80 per cent of all trade, excluding trade involving members of the communist bloc.[42] It is this economic strength which has seemed to many scholars, as we have seen, the basis for designating the USA an empire in the later twentieth century. This economic dimension must, therefore, be discussed in any consideration of US imperialism, especially with respect to the relationship between the domestic and foreign dimensions of this issue.

US ECONOMIC IMPERIALISM[43]

Trade policy between the USA and the rest of the world has fluctuated during the post-World War II period. Recently the USA has adopted a so-called 'aggressive unilateralist' approach to trade policy.[44] This approach is characterised by the Trade Act of 1988 which included the well-known Clause 301. Clause 301 expanded the definition of unfair trade, and complied a list of defaulting nations, which included Japan, India and Brazil. Japan and Brazil were later deleted from this list but, nevertheless, some commentators believed that the US attitude to trade in the 1990s had become fixed. Pierre Martin has also identified the 'aggressive unilateralist' approach in the Western European arena. Even before the Uruguay Round of the GATT talks, the USA had made attempts to halt the EU's subsidisation of grain production by subsidising its own producers, hoping to force the EU into negotiation.

In most of the post-World War II period, however, it has been through the multinational corporation (MNC) that the USA has had most global economic influence. Kiyoshi Kojima has argued that the unprecedented levels of foreign investment on the part of the USA actually discouraged international trade.[45] Until the 1960s, US-based MNCs were largely unchallenged by other national economies and MNCs based in other countries. Indeed, their dominance lasted until the mid-1970s.[46]

The economic strength of the USA, and its economic leadership of the Bretton Woods System, ensured a supportive environment for American-based MNCs. In the context of the Cold War, MNCs were instrumental in ensuring that the non-communist world was committed to capitalism. Before many countries' oil industries were nationalised in the early 1970s, the MNCs were vital vehicles for keeping open the flow of oil from the Middle East to the USA. Later on, the US government came to see the MNCs as important sources of foreign capital exchange, which was necessary to maintain the global role of the USA.[47] Consequently, American political leaders were prepared to give direct foreign investment virtually unequivocal support. These overseas activities by US-based MNCs were, therefore, approved and assisted by the US government, at least in general terms.

US-based MNCs were able to make heavy investments in Europe as tariff barriers went up around the borders of the European Economic Community. In 1950 US direct investment abroad was $11.8 billion; by 1984 it was approximately $233.4 billion.[48] Even by 1969, American-based MNCs produced approximately $140 billion worth of goods: this made their combined production more than any national economies, except those of the Soviet Union and the USA itself.[49]

Arguably, US-based MNCs have been most influential in developing countries – the usual 'targets' for overseas imperialism in the modern world – where high tariff walls have actively encouraged direct foreign investment as a way of overcoming these external barriers. Here, they have faced the most criticism. MNCs are accused of encouraging 'branch plant' economies: those where the developing 'host' country always defers to the industrialised 'home' country, just as the 'branch' or subsidiary of the MNC defers to the locus of the parent company. MNCs are also accused of causing unemployment in the 'host' country because of their lack of labour-intensive production methods.

The analysts of so-called American economic 'decline', have seen the MNCs as passing on sophisticated US technology for what amounts to very little in return. Conversely, other critics of MNCs have claimed to identify a failure on the part of MNCs to transfer technological knowledge or organisational skills, and have accused them of preventing the development of the 'host' country. These critics see the MNCs as retaining their profits for the benefit of their 'home' country. Where profits are invested in the development of the 'host' economy, these critics charge that they are distributed unequitably, and result in the dislocation of both the society and economy of the 'host' country. Gilpin points out, however, that 'one must note that economic growth itself tends to create disparities of wealth'.[50] The evidence that MNCs significantly distort or damage the economies of developing countries is inconclusive.

There is, perhaps, a more severe charge against direct foreign investment by the USA, and especially the activities of US-based MNCs. This is the charge that the widespread presence of MNCs has sometimes resulted in 'host' countries becoming cultural and political 'colonies' of the USA. Certainly, advertising on the part of MNCs encourages the transformation of local traditions and values, and their substitution with American popular culture. The desire to retain the direct investment also acts as a restraint on the political development of the 'host' country. There is an increased pressure for the government of that country to pass laws and draft policies in keeping with US political objectives. Nevertheless, Gilpin again makes the point that the transformation of a society's attitudes and aspirations is the essence of development.[51]

Turning to the economic relationship between the USA and specific regions, we can see a complex economic relationship between the USA and Latin America. Of course, the dynamics of this relationship occur in the context of the international economy. Nevertheless, the USA can be seen, at various times throughout the twentieth century, to be exercising informal economic imperialism towards Latin America. Initially, the American government was concerned only for the raw materials (usually rubber and quartz) which were to be found in Latin America. In 1947 the Rio Treaty, although primarily a defence treaty, laid the foundation for US economic policy toward Latin America in the Cold War era. Unlike its economic policy in Europe, the USA declined to provide a 'Marshall Aid' for Latin America. It also discouraged the states of this continent from joining a proposed International Trade Organisation (ITO), which would have attempted to stabilise the price of raw materials in Latin America. In 1948 the Pan-American Union was re-named the Organisation of American States (OAS), which, according to Nef, 'constituted hardly more than the public relations wrapping of the Rio Treaty, which increasingly served as a vehicle to give American domination a new ideological justification'.[52]

Throughout the Cold War the USA linked economic policy to Latin America with political objectives. At the end of the Cold War there was a general drop in foreign investment in Latin America, including investment from the USA. By 1993, however, the USA was benefiting from the economic recovery in Latin America. The USA had a positive balance of trade with Mexico (US $2,082) in 1993; indeed it was the principal source of Mexican imports.[53]

According to Nef, there has been a general increase in the role in Latin America of such international agencies as the International Monetary Fund (IMF), the World Bank, and the Inter-American Development Bank. The USA has the ability, and the inclination, to manipulate these agencies. An example of such manipulation is the way Chile, Mexico, Venezuela and Costa Rica have been allowed access to loans in return for 'good behaviour'. The corollary of this trend is that these countries become more attractive to foreign (primarily American) investors.

In 1990 Bush announced his Enterprise for the Americas Initiative (EAI). This had three component parts. Firstly, it proposed that bilateral debts between Latin American countries and the USA be partially written off. Secondly, it proposed the creation of a development fund for the region, to be administered by the Inter-American Development Bank (IDB). Bush suggested that the USA would contribute US $100m per year, providing other industrialised countries did the same. Thirdly, and most importantly, however, the EAI envisaged that the Americas might eventually form a trading bloc. This was an indirect response to the formalisation of European integration, due to take place in December 1992. The Initiative's effectiveness has largely been limited to the development of a regular dialogue (around a common agenda) between the political elites of the member countries. Moves towards the development of a pan-American trading bloc have not been taken, nor are they likely to be in the immediate future. Since more than 50 per cent of the US exports to Latin America go to Mexico, NAFTA (the North American Free Trade Agreement) serves, at least for the moment, the needs of the USA regarding free enterprise in the Americas.[54]

This brings us to the relationship between the US economy and its northern neighbour, Canada.[55] Since Confederation in 1867, the government of Canada has felt US economic policies to be imperialistic. The US exploitation of the geographical and economic position of Canada has resulted in an asymmetrical relationship, characterised by fluctuating Canadian dependence on the USA. Ironically, however, in the 1860s the New England states sought protectionist measures against eastern Canadian goods, particularly fish products, which flooded their markets. In 1874 the American Senate was still nervous enough of Canadian trade to refuse to ratify a free trade treaty. The American reluctance to accept Canadian goods proved to be one of the pressures towards Canadian Confederation: the need to ensure a reliable domestic market for Canadian goods.

Under British rule the Canadian economy was not encouraged to develop a manufacturing base. Instead, it remained a resource-based

economy. When the British started to withdraw from Canada, therefore, the Canadians inevitably looked to their southern neighbour for
economic assistance. In 1854 the British government negotiated a
Reciprocity Treaty between the USA and British North America. It
was short-lived, being abrogated in 1866 by the USA. Nevertheless,
reciprocity allowed the USA to encourage Canadian dependence on
trade between the two countries. By the end of the nineteenth century
many American companies had established branch plants in Canada as
a way of jumping the tariff wall (usually 25-30 per cent) which the
Canadian government, under MacDonald, had raised around American
goods. By 1911 trade with the USA was so important that the General
Election of that year severely polarised the Western provinces from
Central Canada. The Western provinces believed the tariffs were detrimental to their livelihood, and wanted free trade with the USA. Central Canada saw protectionism as a necessary buffer against American
imperialism.

Until the early 1980s the US economy exercised what some have
called 'creeping imperialism' in Canada. Both direct and indirect investment by American companies increased. American media products
were increasingly available in Canada. Influence was, however, medi-
ated by selective protectionism. The greatest beneficiaries as far as the
USA was concerned were the defence industries. The perceived Cold
War threat of the Soviet Union precipitated an integration of US and
Canadian defence industries, thus drawing the Canadian economy into
the realm of American security policy.

In 1984, however, Prime Minister Mulroney dismantled the Foreign
Investment Review Agency (FIRA) which had been set up in 1974 to
screen potential investors in Canada. The establishment of 'Investment
Canada' in the place of FIRA was a prelude to the 1989 Free Trade
Agreement (FTA). This allowed for the removal of tariff and non-
tariff barriers between the USA and Canada.

As a partial result of the FTA (in 1994 the FTA was subsumed into
NAFTA) 21.5 per cent of the USA's exports found their way into
Canada in 1989.[56] Moreover, this percentage is rising rapidly.[57] Conversely, in 1990 a staggering 75.5 per cent of Canada's exports were
sold to the USA: 68 per cent of these were in the form of unprocessed
or semi-processed goods, an abnormally high percentage for a developed country; the figure would usually be in the region of 40–50 per
cent. Canada's economic dependence on the USA was such that in
1991 64 per cent of its imports were from that country.[58]

AMERICAN IMPERIALISM IN FOREIGN POLICY[59]

Although many have looked to such economic aspects of the US global role as an indication of informal imperialism, and this may be, to some extent, justified, the classic source of imperialistic behaviour in the history of states is in their foreign policy.

American political imperialism has often been seen as evidenced by US foreign policy-making throughout the twentieth century. In 1947 Marshall Aid was given to Europe, which was linked to the Truman Doctrine. This aid-programme had well-defined political objectives, namely the prevention of the spread of communism to countries outside of the Soviet sphere of influence. In the words of Truman himself, Marshall Aid and the Truman Doctrine were 'two halves of the same walnut'.[60] The Soviet Union did not participate in the provision of aid to Western Europe, as the USA had made sure that the proposals for a revived German economy would be unpalatable to both Molotov and Stalin. Large numbers of American troops were stationed in Western Europe throughout the Cold War period, which had the effect not only of defending US (and Western European) security interests, but also of maintaining a level of American influence. According to Croker:

> What we are dealing with in the US military is not an industrial complex, but a political community, the Army in particular, which links the USA and Europe in an Atlantic community, that enables the political leadership in the USA to manage the transatlantic bargain . . . The Seventh Army provides a cultural underpinning of the American commitment to Europe's defence.[61]

'Security considerations' could have other effects. In 1981–82 Reagan put pressure on Western European and US companies operating in Europe, urging them not to help the Soviet Union build a pipeline to the West for the delivery of natural gas. This pressure, although it was unsuccessful, was widely seen as an attempt on the part of the American President to apply US law outside the territory of the USA.[62]

In Latin America there is even more evidence for the intervention of the USA in domestic political affairs. In the 1930s the USA was concerned about the spread of fascism in Latin America, and began to develop a view of the continent as a military security zone for the USA. During World War II the Americans achieved neutrality from the states of the Pan-American Union. In the Cold War the USA followed this up by being instrumental in the overthrow of several regimes deemed to be 'unfriendly' to its own government. For example, in 1954 it helped to overthrow the elected President of Guatemala, Jacobo Arbenz, and, in 1959, observed the Cuban Revolution with unease. After Castro declared himself to be a Marxist–Leninist in 1960, the USA adopted increasingly interventionist strategies in Cuba too. The disastrous attempted invasion at the Bay of Pigs in 1961 did not deter Kennedy from making a strong stand against the attempted placing of Soviet missiles on the island the following year. Ironically, since the Cuban Missile Crisis, the USA has pursued an anti-imperialist policy in Cuba, breaking off all political and economic links. While the Cuban example is well-known, it is not the only case of US political intervention in the 1960s: in 1964, for instance, the USA supported a coup in Brazil and maintained a right-wing dictatorship there. The following year, it made a similar intervention in the Dominican Republic.

Kennedy also introduced the 'Alliance for Progress' to Latin America. A sort of belated 'Marshall Aid', this was designed to encourage Latin American economic development and so to deter unrest and potential communist upsurges. It also had an attendant political agenda, however, in that it introduced Latin American armies to US methods of 'counter-insurgency' and made them dependent upon the Pentagon for training. American defence companies had to provide their equipment and the spare parts to maintain it, forming another type of dependent relationship.

Under Nixon there was a vehement rejection of reformist proposals put forward by a Committee of Ministers of Economic and Foreign Relations of Latin America. There was no attempt to support the vast majority of reformist measures which had been instigated in the 1950s, and Kennedy's 'Alliance for Progress' was not continued. Instead, the USA encouraged repressive military regimes, on the grounds that they were necessary for the defence of both Latin America and the USA from the Soviet threat.

The emphasis on intervention as a means of resolving 'security issues' continued through to the Reagan Presidency. Reagan felt it necessary for the USA to intervene in the 'Wars of National Liberation' in Nicaragua and El Salvador in 1978–79. He sent 'advisers' to Honduras and El Salvador and rejected the negotiated end to the civil war in El Salvador: his objective of removing the Sandinista government from power seemingly overshadowed all other interests in the region. In 1983 Grenada was invaded by the USA, to almost unanimous condemnation from the rest of the world, including the UK.

Throughout the twentieth century, then, US interests in Latin America revolved around the need to secure that continent as an American 'sphere of influence'. Successive US governments, almost without exception, encouraged the re-militarisation of Latin American states, and replaced left-wing governments with military-dominated authoritarian regimes. Tellingly, the 1987 Acapulco Commitment for Peace, Development and Democracy was quietly dropped by the US government when the Cold War ended, and Latin America was perceived not to be a priority issue in the security of the USA.

Canada has been somewhat more successfully integrated into the security system of the USA. Paradoxically, Canada has needed to achieve a degree of military support from the USA to reduce the possibility of annexation. Indeed, the complexities of neo-imperialist relationships in the twentieth century have meant that the dependent countries have become more given to accepting the current situation; their short-term gains are not usually seen in the context of likely long-term losses.[63] During the Cold War the USA was able to exploit Canada's need of support, and use it – along with Latin America – for its own security purposes. The North American Air Defence Treaty (NORAD), for example, was signed in 1958. This was a political initiative of the USA, and the USA provided 90 per cent of the financial backing for the Treaty. In 1959 the USA signed, with Canada, the Defence Production Sharing Agreement (DPSA); this created 12,000 jobs in Canada, but they were mainly in American branch plants, and dependent upon the American economic advantage of these being located in Canada.

CULTURAL IMPERIALISM

US informal imperialism in Canada can also be seen in the communications industries and it is Canada which gives us the most clear-cut evidence of US cultural imperialism from the Americas. American magazines, television and radio stations have all been accused of penetrating the Canadian market at the expense of Canadian culture.

By 1955 only 20 per cent of the consumer magazines read in Canada were Canadian, and many Canadian-produced magazines had gone out of business.[64] Cultural penetration has become easier since the ratification of the FTA in 1989. The cheapness of American television programmes, particularly light entertainment programmes, acts as a disincentive for the Canadian media to produce their own. Instead, Canadian media companies are able to make easy profits by purchasing the rights to distribute American programmes in Canada.[65]

Cultural imperialism does not automatically mean that other forms of imperialism are present: for example, it does not necessitate US economic imperialism. The profits Canadian companies make out of American programmes are often kept within Canada. For instance, most of the before-tax profit of US $36 million made by the Canadian cable industry in 1976 did not filter back to the USA.[66]

Neither is cultural imperialism equally deeply entrenched in all parts of the Canadian population; the most resistant Canadian barrier to US cultural imperialism is Quebec. Here, media companies are reluctant to import television programmes, even from French-speaking countries. In English-speaking Canada, however, particularly along the USA–Canada border where the population of Canada is concentrated, there is little resistance to US culture. Radio stations have been set up in northern Washington state especially to broadcast into Canada. Even if Canadians wanted to shut out such signals, these are difficult to block, and there is little inclination to do so, since most Canadians are assimilated into American culture.

As is well-known, American cultural imperialism is not merely a regional, but a global phenomenon.[67] Interestingly, the penetration of American popular culture into Latin America took place first among the lower classes of society in the 1930s, while the social elite was absorbed in French culture. This exacerbated the division between the elite and the remainder of the population, and, arguably, contributed to the social problems faced in contemporary Latin America.[68]

The cultural dimension of economics is a node of linkage between the spheres of cultural and economic imperialism. To give an example, the USA has actively exported its style of organisation and methods of business: its 'business culture'. There were 78 business schools in the USA in the 1960s. By 1990 this number had risen to 249, compared with 35 in Canada, 38 in the United Kingdom, and just 3 in Germany.[69] In 1989–90, 23.7 per cent of all Masters degrees awarded were American MBAs.[70]

In global terms, US cultural imperialism can be shown by the spread of English. Along with education, which extends far beyond the area of business studies, the English language is being exported from the USA at an increasing rate. There has been an increase of 40 per cent in the use of English as a foreign language since the 1950s.[71]

Over two-thirds of the world's scientists write in English. Three-quarters of the world's mail is written in English. Of all the information stored in electronic retrieval systems, 80 per cent is stored in English.[72]

It is important to note that it is 'American English' which accounts for much of the growth of the language.

In all of these spheres of activity it is, therefore, possible to see the USA as an empire. Yet the linkage between domestic and foreign affairs is plainly very close, and the characteristics of a formal empire are only undeniably exhibited in relation to the domestic affairs of the USA. This is especially clear in the case of territorial imperialism, which can only be attested on the North American continent and has, in the past, been shown in relation to a few small overseas territories, most of which are now parts of the US federal structure. The division between formal and informal imperialism (discussed earlier in this chapter) may provide a useful means of understanding this situation, if we consider the USA itself to be a 'formal' imperial 'core', which may be classed as an empire, with an 'informal' periphery, in which aspects of political, economic and cultural imperialism, but not true empire, can be identified as being present, albeit in a 'patchy' and often short-lived fashion.

AN EMPIRE IN DECLINE?

If the USA is an empire, is it an empire in decline? The crucial question of defining what is meant by 'US decline' can be addressed in many ways. To some, it has been answered simply in terms of the changes taking place in the US economy, in relation to that of the Asia–Pacific area or of Europe. To others, US decline has been seen in strictly military terms, the loss of pre-eminence in terms of weapons, military training, tactical, or strategic, advantages. Another approach is to take US decline as demonstrated by America's position in international politics, in relation to its allies and opponents in terms of policy and leadership.

Yet, in order to define 'decline' one has to be able to set out a reference point from which decline may have taken place, and to ask: 'decline in what terms?' One must also differentiate between decline, collapse, loss of presumed status and crisis. Most of these distinctions are absent from many discussions of the current and immediate future prospects of the USA. There tends to be an assumption that decline is equivalent to collapse, that loss of 'superpower' status means that the USA will imminently become a 'Third World' state.

Here, these categories will be kept apart and a simple definition of 'decline' will be adopted as follows: US decline can be evaluated in terms of the extent to which the US government is unable to achieve its foreign and domestic policy aims, to retain its role as the 'lone superpower' that it held at the end of the Gulf War in 1991, to play a military, economic, political and cultural 'leadership role' among its allies as it did at the end of the Cold War, and to maintain its own domestic stability and territorial integrity. The reference point for these criteria, from which decline in all of these respects may be identified, is the end of the Gulf War and, more specifically, George Bush's 'New World Order' speech. This point, it will be argued, marked the height of US political and military dominance in international affairs.

As this view makes no essential equation between state-collapse and decline, although it admits that decline in this sense could eventually produce state-collapse, the term 'relative decline' will be used here. This is also more suitable when discussing the USA in the present and near future, because one is examining decline in relation to a pre-decided level or point.

THE USA AS A DECLINING EMPIRE: A COMPARATIVE VIEW

If the USA can be reclassified as an imperial state then the question of relative decline can be seen in a new context. First, it may be examined in terms which place far more importance on US domestic affairs than have all other analyses of this question (an approach which will form the basis of the next chapter) because the American empire exists within, not outside, the USA. A relative decline in informal imperial activity in the periphery may not be equivalent to relative decline in the formal empire itself. Second, it can be seen in a comparative context of the general decline of imperialism in the twentieth century. This will form the final topic in this chapter.

The nineteenth century was dominated by European empires. The British, French, Belgian, Portuguese and Dutch empires all survived until the mid–late twentieth century in some form. These empires were each the result of European territorial expansion during the period 1500–1900. Outside Western Europe, the Russian, Chinese and Japanese empires all persisted into the twentieth century, even if, in the case of Russia and China, supposedly 'anti-imperialistic' communist governments had taken control of their administration.

Communism did not in any case lead to lasting decolonisation: the Russian and Chinese empires were maintained by the communist rulers. Consequently, it is possible (as already mentioned, now conventional among scholars of international relations) to write of a 'Russian empire' existing continuously from the Tsarist through the communist period of Russian history. Likewise the Chinese empire was not dissolved by Mao Zedong or his successors, and still survives in the 1990s. While World War II brought about the collapse of the Japanese empire and of the final twentieth-century attempt to establish a German empire through armed aggression against its neighbours, the same War afforded the Russians an opportunity for what are usually seen as new additions to their sphere of influence or even direct control.

In Western Europe, World War II had a less direct effect on the survival of imperialism, but the post-War period was characterised by widespread decolonisation by the Western European states. Although an indirect effect of the War, in the case of the UK and France this had a major and direct impact on the colonies of these states. This left Russia and China as the only Eurasian empires.

This short account of imperial history forms the context of an examination of the USA in relation to the other twentieth century empires. It highlights one central fact about the surviving empires in existence in the 1970s and 1980s, in contrast to those of the 1920s and 1930s: both Russia and China incorporated contiguous territories into the core state, rather than maintaining distant colonies which were territorially detached from the core area. In both empires the ideology of the state made it clear that inhabitants of these colonial regions were to consider themselves full citizens of the state (a tactic already employed in the nineteenth and twentieth centuries by the French and British), and promoted the adoption of the language and aspects of the culture of the core state in these colonies. Consequently, the situation in Kazakhstan in the Stalinist period was analogous to that in 'Chinese' Manchuria in the 1970s, in these respects. The rise of these 'unitary territorial empires' in contrast to the 'maritime empires' of the nineteenth century can be seen, without any reference to the case of the USA, to be the overwhelming change in the character of imperialism in the later twentieth century.

Looking at the USA in this context enables us to place it more exactly in the history of imperialism. It too was formed, as we have seen, as a result of the conquest by Europeans of extra-European territories and involved the translation of a cosmopolitan European culture and a European language to another continent. In this respect the analogy is with the British and French empires of the nineteenth centuries and before.

The most important comparison is, however, with these two other unitary territorial empires (Russia and China) with which it shares all the key defining characteristics. For this purpose, it is not important that the USA adopted a form of liberal democracy and held freedom and free-market economics as fundamental political ideals (so did France and Britain in their imperial phases) or that the formation of the American state too had resulted from colonisation. It was not alone in being an ex-colony with its own empire: this was already the case in Latin America.

Seen in this way, the USA can be grouped, in this respect, with the other two most successful empires of the post-World War II period: Soviet Russia and China. As such, this casts the Cold War into a new context, as a confrontation between rival empires each seeking global hegemony or at least the annihilation in political terms of its imperial rivals.[73]

Consequently, an alternative picture to that usually given of international politics between 1945 and the present can be outlined. In this alternative view, the post-World War II period still saw competition between empires, each holding a sphere of influence in which middle-ranking and lesser states aligned themselves with the most successful and militarily strongest of the War's imperial victors. This places the later twentieth century in a different historical context to that usually proposed, for the alleged uniqueness of the Cold War vanishes in comparison with a series of such bipolar imperial confrontations and groups of aligned secondary actors, from the Roman:Persian stand-off in the Middle East in the third–seventh centuries to World War I.[74] Obviously, differences of technology and geographical scale have affected each of these confrontations so that none is exactly comparable, but the pattern seems historically attested in every century for which records exist and in which an inter-state system is definable.

This brings us to the question of US decline. As is well-known, this has been a topic of heated debate among both American and European political scientists and historians since Paul Kennedy first brought the issue to a wide audience in his monumental *The Rise and Fall of the Great Powers* in 1987.

Kennedy's thesis is straightforward in outline. Linking economic and military 'power' he suggests that the USA will shortly become a far less important international actor than at present. In his original work this was seen as representing the economic outstripping of the USA by Japan, although recently he has tended to view the European Union (EU) as a potential successor to the USA's leading economic role. By equating economic and military 'power' with political pre-eminence, Kennedy is able to quantify the extent of national 'power' in a fashion seldom attempted in non-economic terms since the end of the behaviouralist phase of international relations scholarship.

The key problem with the 'Kennedy thesis', which has been highlighted by subsequent studies and by subsequent events, is that Kennedy failed to predict the end of both the Cold War and the Soviet Union. An equally serious problem is his simplistic equation between economic and military might, and between both of these characteristics and the 'power' of a state. These are hardly errors which can be attributed to Kennedy alone; they are part of the materialist mainstream of approaches to change in contemporary political economy. This has frequently been far less political than economic in its content, involving little more than a consideration of the economic aspects of policy and the implications for political action of economic choice and events.

If one re-emphasises the political aspect and sees economic relations as integrated with and structured by political factors, then a different relationship between political and economic 'power' can be seen to exist. In this new relationship, the political 'power' of an actor is not dependent on its economic might; rather the reverse is true.

In this context it may protested that the rise of the USA as an economic force in the global system occurred prior to its emergence as a political 'great power', but this is not so if one adopts the interpretation of US expansion proposed earlier in this chapter. According to this view, the US was already an imperial 'power' before 1900, when it overtook the UK in economic terms. Moreover, US economic growth occurred as a result of its imperial market (usually supposed to be a domestic market) within the American state itself. The growth in the US global economy in contrast to the decline of the European share of the global market can be seen in this context also, as the relative success of the US empire in competing with the European empires (and finally seeing all of them topple) during the course of the twentieth century.

Another failing noticeable in Kennedy's work is the lack of account of recent work on transnational actors in international affairs. Again, given Kennedy's terms of reference this is to some extent understandable – he makes it clear that he writes very much as a historian of the modern world rather than a political scientist.

One cannot escape noticing that there is no reference to multinational corporations in the index to his book. They do play a role in his considerations but, like the part given to domestic factors, their role is very much marginal to his main concern. To some extent this is simply a difference of approach, but the problem which it causes also undermines the utility of Kennedy's analysis of the USA.

The post-War world has seen an unprecedented rise in the number (if not importance) of international non-state actors. Many of these actors have been based in and operated from the USA, and many are part of domestic US society and economics as much as the global reach of the US economy. A further neglected dimension, the consequences of globalisation for the USA, relates to the same issue. The distinction between domestic and international affairs is inevitably undermined for those members of a society which participate, through telecommunications, in global rather than local exchanges.

CONTRASTING VIEWS OF US DECLINE: RESPONSES TO THE 'KENNEDY THESIS'

Paul Kennedy's book remained on the US best-seller list for 34 weeks when it was first published, and prompted a broad and intense debate over US decline.[75] This was, arguably, especially vigorous because many US scholars might be said to exhibit somewhat greater patriotism than their European counterparts. While, for instance, many British scholars would align themselves with Marxist, internationalist, socialist and other radical viewpoints in discussing the, then contemporary, decline of British imperialism in the period from 1900 to 1970, the radical tradition of US scholarship is countered by a more conservative alternative.

Consequently, the suggestion that the USA was about to lose its pre-eminence resulted in a strong defence mounted by US academics and others, which was combined with a broader and less 'politically-charged' debate among the scholarly community internationally. Before considering the reality – or not – of US decline, we shall, therefore, provide a very brief overview of the opinions of these scholars who disagreed (as we do) with the Kennedy thesis, and those who supported or opposed the view that the USA was in decline.

We shall begin with the stances taken by two scholars for whom we have especial respect, yet with whom we disagree in regard to the question of US decline: Susan Strange and Joseph Nye. Kennedy's book was published in 1987; the following year Strange's article, 'The Persistent Myth of Lost Hegemony', persuasively argued that the USA retained 'structural power' in the world economy, despite a decline from its economic dominance of the late 1940s.[76] At the time, Strange was probably correct, and US military fortunes were at their height for the next few years (in 1989–91) with the collapse of the Soviet Union. But there seems much to commend Garnham's re-analysis of

1990, that by that time US economic fortunes had suffered a major setback.[77] This is even more acute today, as Kegley and Raymond have pointed out: the Reagan period left the USA debt-ridden.[78] Today, the USA has shifted status from the largest global creditor to largest global debtor nation.' So, although if it were 1988 it would be possible to agree with Strange on this question, it is more difficult to do so in 1996.

In her most recent contribution to this debate, Susan Strange maintains the view that the USA is not in decline, considering it a 'special case' to which historical precedents are inapplicable.[79] This is a more problematical view, perhaps, in that almost any historical entity – certainly any state – could be described as in one sense a 'special case'. As no two periods of history, or events, can theoretically be identical in every respect, all historical cases must necessarily be 'special'.

The question is rather one of the degree of 'specialness' involved, and the extent to which one believes that historical generalisation is possible. So, it is essential to understand exactly what she means by the 'specialness' of the USA.

In her definition – explicitly stated in her paper – the special characteristics of the USA are twofold: it is based on 'legitimacy' which 'depends hardly at all on blood and ethnicity but on nationality voluntarily acquired by multi-ethnic immigrants',[80] and other states expect far more of it (as a global arbitrator and stabiliser) than they have of any previous actor. The first of these points seems at least debatable as grounds for American 'specialness': one immediately recalls that the Roman empire, also, was not based on blood or ethnicity (anyone potentially could, and often did, acquire citizenship and *romanitas* after the third century AD, when all freeborn people in the empire were officially citizens from birth). There was far less uniting these people than can be held in common by citizens of modern America – communication problems alone saw to that! So America is certainly not 'special' in this respect, in relation to at least one of the historical analogies which one might bring to bear in discussing the rise and fall of states and empires.

Strange's second argument for specialness may have more to commend it: there has been a high expectation of the USA by other significant global actors since the start of the 1990s. But does international perception decree national 'specialness'? It is uncertain whether this is the case. Perceptions cannot fundamentally change the internal structure or culture of a state easily, and there are stronger indications that US perceptions and culture are still acting to transform the international politics of other states (we do not suppose America so weak already as to doubt this) than vice versa.

Strange argues compellingly, however, that the structural context of international political economy in the late twentieth century is fundamentally changed from that of earlier centuries. But it is the late twentieth century, not the USA, which is (in this respect) historically unique. No earlier period had access to the technological innovations available to the late twentieth-century world and these have permitted economic and other exchanges of types previously unknown. In turn, these have internationalised important aspects of economic activity. It may be doubted, as we shall see, whether this changed context of global political economy acts to enhance, or undermine, the stability of the USA and its pre-eminent role in international affairs. It may make US decline more likely to be globally significant and detrimental to international stability, but not less likely.

This brings us to Nye's interpretation.[81] Nye argues that 'the new world order will not be an era of American hegemony'[82] but Nye doubts that the USA is in decline, instead seeing the concern felt in the contemporary USA as a type of recurrent national self-doubt. While one may agree with Nye both on the 'New World Order' and American self-doubt, he argues that this self-doubt is among the greatest threats to the USA and is ill-founded in current international politics. Here we must part company with him, for if national self-doubt was to be found in the USA since the early days of the Republic, and if it is so destructive, why has it not stopped the USA from rising to such prominence? Our reasons for doubting that empirical grounds overall support the stability of the USA's premier position in world politics will become clear later.

Strange and Nye have not been alone in proposing differing interpretations of the debate initiated by Kennedy, and this debate is, as yet, unresolved in the USA and elsewhere, but two crucial characteristics may be pointed out at this stage. The debate, like that regarding US imperialism, has concentrated almost entirely upon issues of international political economy and on foreign policy or security matters. It has tended to overlook both domestic factors and the continental context of the USA. Perhaps scholars have felt these to be irrelevant, especially in a supposedly 'globalised' world.

So, while it is impossible to credit the 'Kennedy thesis', this does not necessarily discredit the view that the USA is in relative decline. The question, from the standpoint taken in this work is, of course, somewhat different from that addressed by Kennedy, in that here the

USA is seen as an imperial state. The question of decline has, therefore, to be examined in those terms: does the American empire show traces of decline? As this empire is founded on control of the North American continent itself, one must therefore seek traces of that decline in America as well as in the international arena. This approach also makes it possible to escape from the sharp division between domestic and international politics made in Kennedy's work (although this is less acute in his later book) and to stress the role of transnational and linking relationships which connect the domestic and international spheres. An alternative approach to the evaluation of US decline can be derived from a comparative perspective. If we employ the model of the USA as an internal empire, founded on and contained within the 'New World', it is possible to compare its rise and potential decline with those of other empires in the twentieth century.

In a classic study of post-medieval imperialism, Bergesen and Schoenberg attempted to assess the extent of imperialism through time since 1500.[83] This data was reworked by Taylor into a cyclical model of imperialism, in which two long cycles (1500–1800 and 1800–1950) can be detected.[84] This cyclical patterning has also been detected in an independent study conducted by Dark, which noted a 400-year cycle of rise and decline in international systems.[85] This suggests a cycle of rise and decline in the post-medieval international system between 1600 and 2000, and apparently another such cycle, starting in 1800 and potentially persisting until 2200.

Although to some extent these studies address different issues and result in somewhat different patterns, they are closely comparable in that each sees the emergence of a post-medieval international order which persisted until the present but is now in sharp decline. They may be correlated if one notes that Taylor's cycles of imperialism consider political units – empires – within the international systems examined by Dark's model. That is, the potential exists for both patterns to be drawn together into a single model of the rise and fall of empires and international systems, if we see the rise and fall of imperialism as occurring within, but closely related to, the rise and fall of international systems. At this point, the relevance to the contemporary USA will become clear. If these cycles of long-term systemic change exist, then the present international order incorporates two patterns. One sees the order which has persisted since *c.*1600 (the 'Westphalian system') in steep decline but, more importantly here, the other suggests that *c.*1800 marked the origin of a new international system. It would seem that this was dominated by a fresh set of imperial states.

These states, according to both of these models, include the classic imperialist states of the nineteenth century. According to the second of these views, the contemporary international system is also characterised by the rise of the USA, and by the increasing dominance of the USA in that system through the twentieth century. This last observation brings in another thread in recent theoretical studies of the rise and fall of states and international systems: the work of George Modelski.[86] Modelski has argued for the existence of long-cycles in world politics in which patterns of events characterise a series of repeated surges in the growth and decline of 'great powers'. This view incorporates the perspective that the nineteenth century was itself dominated by imperial dominance, and that the twentieth century has seen the rise of the USA to such a position. According to Modelski, the USA entered a phase of decline following the Vietnam War.

All of these studies agree on several points. The international system that has existed since the seventeenth century is in decline, and imperialism has been a key element of this system. Combined, they suggest that the successor system emerged in *c.*1800, and that this was also connected to the emergence and decline of empires.

To relate these perspectives to the question of US decline, it is possible to suggest that, on these grounds alone, the USA is part of a system which is beginning to decline. This decline is likely, according to at least two separate independent studies of long-term systemic change. These studies also suggest that the chronological relationship between the decline of European empires and the decline of the system established in *c.*1600 is very close. That is, the phase of imperialism begun in *c.*1600 began to decline when the system itself went into decline. If so, the phase which began in *c.*1800 may be expected to begin to decline after *c.*2000. As Taylor notes, the exact chronology of this decline was different in different 'core states', but the pattern is consistent throughout the system.

If the USA is an empire, founded in *c.*1800, then its decline in the last decades of the twentieth century (and early in the twenty-first century) can be expected on comparative historical grounds alone. By combining these three independent and distinct threads of analysis derived from long-term studies of the international system, therefore, it is possible to demonstrate strong grounds for postulating US decline in the final decade of the present century or in the first decades of the next century. It is important to note, however, that this decline is to be expected in relative terms, and does not necessarily mean that state-collapse or national disintegration are likely to occur.

It is possible to go beyond this comparative and theoretical conclusion by relating this argument to the observation made earlier concerning the rise of unitary territorial empires (China, the Soviet Union and the USA) after 1945. This pattern may then be seen in the context of the decline in the principal nineteenth-century empires following 1900. In this interpretation, the World Wars can be understood in terms of a terminal clash of 'nineteenth-century' maritime empires, in which the only surviving empires were those which were not maritime in their geopolitical organisation. The existence of such territorial blocs can, then, be seen to have led to a new clash of empires – the Cold War. In this sense, the Cold War was a form of inter-imperial 'warfare' as it represented a struggle for global supremacy between opposing imperial states. This, in turn, can be seen as the last stage of the pattern of growth and decline of imperialism begun in *c.*1800.

The close correlation between the chronology of previous phases of imperial growth and decline may, therefore, encourage a comparative perspective on this conflict. It is interesting that the conflict of empires has, historically, immediately preceded systemic collapse.[87] This may suggest that the post-Cold War period is one in which the decline of both of the two territorial empires involved in the conflict might be expected to follow their confrontation. Again, in historical terms, such a transformation has tended to occur very rapidly. That this may in fact have happened is supported by the rapid demise of the Russian (communist) empire – the Soviet Union.

The combined studies of these analysts of long-term change in international affairs enable us to build an integrated model of the rise and fall of European imperialism since 1500. They enable us to re-interpret the meaning of the Cold War and of the post-Cold War phase of international politics. They also allow the possibility that there are strong theoretical and comparative grounds to suppose that the relative decline of the USA is already taking place and is likely to accelerate in the remainder of the twentieth century. In the sense that a new international system might be in the process of formation, the claims for a 'New World Order' may also be justified: a system without imperialism for the first time in post-medieval history (unless the Chinese state survives in its present form) and with a post-Westphalian international order may indeed be emerging. But this is not the 'New World Order' envisaged by George Bush.

It will be necessary to return to aspects of these themes in later chapters. It must be stressed, however, that if one is to define the USA as a primarily continental empire – that is, one centred on the imperialism in the 'New World' rather than on the American pursuit of global domination – then one must look at the internal politics of the USA in order to seek direct evidence of its relative decline.

Yet if one is to examine the question of the decline of the American empire in North America, given the comments made above about the attempts to exercise US hegemony in the Americas overall from the nineteenth century until the present, it will be necessary to examine the USA in a wider continental context. These two analyses will form the basis of the next two chapters, and there will be drawn together into a single integrated approach to the question of assessing contemporary trends and their longer term significance.

Interestingly, it will be argued that this context may contribute to, rather than contrast with, the international processes of change which may be detected inside the USA itself. It is central to the understanding of the role of the USA in contemporary international relations to appreciate how closely it is linked to the existing international system. The network of inter-state and transnational linkages which may be taken to constitute the Western international system has, in many respects, been centred on the USA since 1945. America itself has promoted and built up these connections and institutions, incorporating them within its international political strategy and domestic economy.

The end of the Cold War has accentuated the closeness of the relationship between US-based institutions, the US economy, US military forces and the existing international 'order'. In this respect, the American aspiration to create a 'New World Order' after the Gulf War was entirely reasonable as, among all the world's states, only the USA could have hoped to restructure the international system. The transnationalisation of business and the globalisation of US cultural values and norms have also been aspects of this same internationalisation of the USA itself. As the world has become, in a sense, more 'American' during the late twentieth century so America has become more closely linked to the rest of the world. This is often realised, but the implications for changes taking place within the USA have not, perhaps, been fully taken into account in studies of US decline. If US domestic affairs are so closely linked to international affairs, and to the global standing of the USA, then US domestic decline may necessarily lead to US global decline. A crisis in the domestic situation of the USA might have global impacts and affect not only the quality and prosperity of American life 'at home' but also America's role in the international system. Likewise system-wide factors, the broad patterns of growth and decline so far discussed, might be seen to have an equal, or even more accentuated, rather than a diminished, role in the modern world, in comparison to that which they seem to have played in the past.

CONCLUSION

It is, therefore, possible to recognise the USA as an 'internal', continental empire. Founded in the eighteenth century phase of imperial establishment, it has shared a similar pattern of international, large-scale, political development to other post-medieval empires. Like most of those empires, it has pursued many essentially altruistic policies, alongside those of economic expansion and the search for political and military pre-eminence in world affairs.

Following the World Wars, which left the maritime empires of Britain, France, Germany and other states in steep decline, there were only three such empires which retained their position relatively unscathed: America, Russia and China. Of these, the close involvement of America and Russia in the defeat of the Axis and their greater levels of economic strength and military might, compared to China, have long been recognised as key factors in their rise to post-War pre-eminence in global politics. The surviving empires were all characterised by controlling large blocs of territory within their formal borders, and fostering national identity and national unity in the context of strong, state-backed, ideologies. In this context, the way in which the Cold War became a battle not only of states, but also of ideologies and cultures, becomes understandable.

This view enables us to reinterpret the nature of the Cold War, seeing it as, essentially, a conflict between two opposing imperial states (the USA and USSR) along with their allies and informal colonies. Its end may be seen in terms of long-term patterns in the rise and fall of empires and of international systems, explicable on systemic and processual grounds rather than in terms of shorter-term military or economic factors alone. The end of the Cold War and imperial collapse are, therefore, closely linked. This represents not the 'fall of communism' (one remaining empire (China) retains a 'communist' ideology), but the end of an inter-imperial system, following which all former empires are in steep decline as global 'powers'. Both Russia and the USA have ceased to be 'superpowers', in the sense that they are no longer able to continue their Cold War role of dominating hemispheric politics: their status as 'superpowers' was, in part, a product of the Cold War itself. So, in relative terms, a decline in the importance of America in international affairs has occurred since the 1980s and it is reasonable, therefore, to ask whether the decline will continue or whether there will be a period of relative stability regarding its global standing.

2 Domestic Political Instability in North America

As we have seen, the question of whether the USA is in relative decline has almost exclusively been addressed by considering the US role in international affairs.[1] Yet, as we saw in the last chapter, the 'American empire' does not exist as an external so much as a continental regime, although a 'periphery' of informal imperialistic activity can be defined outside the 'core'. So, to examine the question of US decline, one must look at the domestic affairs of the USA itself, and to do so effectively it is interesting to consider it in comparison with Canada, its continental neighbour. It will be seen that many of the processes of change visible in the contemporary USA also exist in Canada and they are, in a few cases, further advanced in Canada than they are in the USA. The prospects for the USA can, therefore, in some such cases, be evaluated in relation to trends already more advanced in Canada. This comparison is made more important by evidence of convergence between the USA and Canada and this, too, will be examined in this chapter.

In making such a survey of trends towards instability in the USA, it must be noted at the outset that our approach is not simply to highlight one aspect or factor of the American way of life, or of the American economy, as a potential source of instability. It is to search for any such trends in whatever sector, rather than to impose a more strict definition of the aspects of contemporary America to be examined.

As such, the aim of this chapter is to highlight trends deriving from regional differences, social inequalities and grievances, ideological and religious change, cultural factors, population movements, and economic decline and disparity. Before attempting to do so, however, the fundamental constitutional differences between the USA and Canada must be outlined, for these at once form a backdrop to much that will be discussed. Deep-seated constitutional variations should not, however, deter us from seeking comparisons between two societies closely linked by geography, economics, cultural and religious factors, and aspects of social organisation and political ideologies. Such differences must, of course, alert us to the problems of inferring that changes occurring in Canada must inevitably take place in the USA, or vice versa, but need not deter us from such a comparative view nor from noting evidence of convergence.

First, however, the different significance which is placed here on the relative importance of economic and social factors, compared to that employed by other scholars, must be noted. This is especially significant, because a re-evaluation of the role of social and cultural change in promoting national decline is a key aspect of this study.

ECONOMIC AND SOCIAL APPROACHES TO THE CONTEMPORARY USA

It is a remarkable aspect of the intellectual history of the late Cold War that, as Marxism collapsed in Eastern Europe, Western scholars came increasingly to see global change in economistic terms.[2] Marx had argued that economic factors underlay processes of change in determining the rise and fall of states, societies, ideologies and cultures. An economic view of change also forms the basis of most recent studies of whether the USA is, or is not declining – and of global change in general – by Kennedy and all those scholars (whose work was considered in Chapter 1) who have attempted to disagree with him. This is curious, especially when most such academics would not consider themselves Marxists, or neo-Marxists, and given the global collapse of Marxist–Leninist ideology.

Here an alternative approach is taken. It is not denied that economic factors play an important part in structuring the resources and options available to any state, both now and in the past, but it is proposed here that far greater significance must be attached to social, cultural, ideological and religious factors and to the developmental context of the state than has been the case in previous studies.

The basis of this view is that societies do not change as if they are machines, but they change because of human decision-making and in response to altered social and cultural, as well as economic, circumstances. Such decisions are made within a social, cultural, ideological and religious matrix of beliefs, perceptions, attitudes and memory. That is, how individuals react to situations is an outcome of who they are and their world view. Their freedom to act as they choose is then structured by other factors, including economic factors, but these are, in turn, the outcome of similar decisions in the past and so partly structured by non-material factors themselves. Consequently, economic change does not 'drive' other transformations; the relationship is more contextual and interactive.

Underlying these dimensions of change one may identify more deep-running historical processes. But again these are not those of economic 'substructure', rather, they derive from the structures by which decisions can be made and information exchanged. In their representation in current affairs they appear as historical forces, structuring general patterns of change rather than determining specifics.

As this book is primarily concerned about short-term changes, those encompassing decades rather than centuries, this social and cognitive context of change must be evaluated in order to offset the over-emphasis on economics (the 'economistic approach') which has characterised other studies. By encompassing and placing primacy on non-economic factors, a more historically valid picture of change can, therefore, be constructed.

To understand trends likely to promote or limit the likelihood of US 'relative decline' in the next half-century, it is necessary to establish the social and cognitive context of political life in the contemporary USA. Changes in culture, social organisation, religious affiliation and attitudes may all be relevant to this question. Economic factors are, of course, a major part of this overall context also, but cannot be separated as an over-riding or fundamental force determining all else. In keeping with the historical perspective and approach of this book, however, it seems appropriate to begin with one of the most enduring aspects of American society and politics: the Constitution itself.

The Constitution of the United States appears remarkably secure – a model of democracy in fact. Changes to the Constitution since it was ratified in March 1789 have been largely minor or cosmetic, the last being the lowering of the voting age in 1971.[3] Reverence of the Constitution is part of the national identity of the USA; acceptance of the constitutional status quo would appear to be a 'given' in contemporary American life. Unlike in Canada, where discontented groups are prone to blame the deficiencies of the Constitution for their woes, in the USA such groups clamour for the existing Constitution to be upheld.

Despite the constitutional unity of the USA, separatist rhetoric can be found in the Southwestern states of California and Texas, but it is absorbed by the political 'mainstream' as a cultural phenomenon, rather than being seen by the majority of the US population as a genuine separatist movement. The importance of this 'regionalist' rhetoric must not, however, be played down; indeed, former Presidents Reagan and

Bush emphasised their Californian and Texan identities to political effect. In view of global trends towards political fragmentation[4] this regionalism may be assigned greater political significance than is often the case in scholarly studies of the USA. Similarly, more widespread trends towards the increased control of international institutions over the internal affairs of states[5] mean that the United States' constitutional stability cannot be assumed to be permanent. It may be worth noting, indeed, that the Roman empire, another unitary territorial empire (and deriving from a Roman Republican empire not constitutionally dissimilar from the United States in some respects) collapsed after hundreds of years of apparent stability.

Historically, however, circumstances have tended to promote US political unity.[6] The USA benefits from the fact that its constituent parts actively petitioned to join the Union and did not have to be persuaded to surrender rights and privileges. For example, the US Constitution had been firmly established for 123 years, and had stood the test of a drawn-out civil war, before Arizona, the 48th state, joined in 1912. It had been in place for 170 years before Alaska and Hawaii joined in 1959. They were in no position to demand special privileges.

Unlike Canada, the United States has not had to contend with strident demands from a region separated from its neighbours by cultural, religious and linguistic allegiances.[7] To give an example, Utah, settled as a Mormon theocracy in 1847, has consistently made its practices congruent with the United States Constitution. When Mormons made the migration from Illinois and Missouri to the unsettled Great Basin, Brigham Young announced their purpose as, 'a foundation for a territorial and state government under the Constitution of the United States, where we shall be the first settlers and a vast majority of the people'. Given this reverence for the Constitution, it was not threatening to the unity of the USA that, although Mormons conform to the 'letter of the law', they do not conform to the 'spirit of the law': they see the law as subordinate to the authority of their religion.[8]

Texas entered the Union in a similarly acquiescent fashion. The American settlers in the Mexican region now known as Texas declared, in 1836, their wish to be independent from Mexico. They achieved independence the same year, gaining 188 Texan 'martyrs' along the way at the Alamo. Although Texas existed as an independent state for a period of nine years, it continued to sue for annexation to the USA, and eventually achieved this in 1845. Interestingly, a similar effort two years earlier had been rejected by the Senate, which had seen the Annexation Treaty simply as an effort to extend slavery into the West.

By 1845, however, the threat that the British might annex Texas before the Americans was too great for Northern Senators to ignore.[9] Californian independence, by contrast, which existed for less than four weeks in June 1846, did not spring from a separatist movement and Californians made little objection to the raising of the American flag in July 1847. Again, this was prompted by fears that the British or French might move towards annexation.

The greatest pressure on the United States Constitution came when not one state but twelve, all adjacent to each other, demanded that they be accorded the right to maintain the 'peculiar institution' of slavery.[10] Countered by abolitionist feeling in the North and abroad, as well as the issue of whether new states in the West should be allowed to keep slaves, the Southern claims to autonomy in this matter were found to be impossible to accommodate. The Civil War of 1861–65 (or the 'War Between the States' as it is still known in parts of the South) claimed more lives than America lost in both of the twentieth-century World Wars. The institutions provided by the state failed to achieve their purpose: political dialogue and Supreme Court jurisdiction were ignored, and unity was maintained by violence.

That inherent characteristic of the Southern states, 'Southern autonomy', was not, however, laid to rest in the aftermath of the Civil War. Northern victory did not bring about the 'more lasting union' many had predicted. Although the time had passed when the Southern states could use violence to settle constitutional disagreement, they were still prepared to unite to challenge the federal government in the 1960s when the civil rights legislation was passed. In 1954 when the Supreme Court precedent decision on segregation was made, the South refused to implement the ruling in favour of de-segregation. In his summing up, the Chief Justice in the '*Brown* v. *The Board of Education, Topeka, Kansas*' decision said,

> To separate [black children] from others of similar age and qualifications solely because of their race generates a feeling of inferiority as to their status in the community that may affect their hearts and minds in a way unlikely ever to be undone.[11]

The case, therefore, was a landmark victory in the drive by Southern blacks to dismantle the 'Jim Crow' laws – laws which forced blacks into separate public accommodation from whites, using the theoretical premise that the facilities were essentially 'separate but equal'.[12] Rather than moving to implement the de-segregation order and prosecute offenders in the state courts, Southern mayors let violence break out in their towns when schools did move to integrate. Intimidation of blacks, including a horrific rise in the number of lynchings, was ignored all over the South. In the infamous incident at Little Rock, Arkansas, the federal government was forced to call out the National Guard when the Governor of Arkansas refused to help black high school students through a barricade around their school. This demonstrated the willingness of these states to assert their autonomy at the expense of national unity and deference to delegated authority. It should also be noted that the other two branches of the federal government, the Executive and the Congress, were also reluctant to either introduce or pass legislation which supported the Supreme Court's ruling. This, too, was a fragmentation of the unity of the United States' institutions of state, demonstrating that constitutional pressure from the South had not slackened, nor was it any easier to assuage.

The prejudice encountered by blacks during the Civil Rights Movement, and the difficulties of getting civil rights legislation passed, not to mention implemented, had the effect, in some areas, of deepening the fissures between the black and white communities in the United States. The movement was not a challenge to the federal system as it stood: civil rights leaders sought to restore to blacks the rights accorded to them in the Reconstruction Amendments of 1868.

Unlike the Québécois in Canada, or some Native American groups, blacks in the mainstream civil rights movement did not want extra protections for their cultural heritage; on the contrary, they wanted to enter the democratic system on the same terms as their fellow citizens. Indeed, recent work on the culture of black Americans in the eighteenth and nineteenth centuries has suggested that in the domestic sphere, as well as in the public sphere of slavery, the majority of black slaves had already been socialised into European culture prior to the abolition of slavery.[13] This is a suggestion approved by those black American soldiers returning from overseas service who testify to having had their 'American-ness' confirmed in them.

For a significant and influential minority of blacks, however, white prejudice and the failure of the civil rights movement to eradicate black poverty, particularly in the Northern ghettos, exacerbated their feelings of alienation from the rhetoric of the Constitution.[14] Merely giving them the same rights as other American citizens was no longer enough. Having been considered 'less than citizens' for longer than America had even existed, some blacks were imbued with a vehement 'black nationalism' which did not correlate with the national feeling as expressed by other Americans. An upsurge in ethnic identification then followed, with blacks rejecting the political culture in which they had just been given leave to participate. Blacks then claimed the legitimation of their own cultural identity, sometimes as 'Africans', sometimes as 'African-Americans' who had a different experience of what it was to be 'American' from that usually articulated by whites. The ensuing 'Black Nationalism' movement led, among others, by Malcolm X, a 'Nation of Islam' leader from Detroit, was not simply a threat to American stability in that it threatened to create pockets of black autonomy. Rather, the pluralistic rhetoric was the most threatening because it renounced the popular perception of what it meant to be 'American'. The question which continues to pose a major dilemma for the USA as a 'pluralist' society is how to vindicate cherished cultures and traditions without breaking the bonds of cohesion – common ideals, political institutions, common language, common culture – that hold the Republic together.

The question has become more complex for, in the same way that peoples in Eastern Europe and the former Soviet Union redirected their allegiance to religious or ethnic groups and renounced communism – causing it to lose its ideological dominance – so, ideological aggression between the West and the former communist bloc ceased. In the case of the United States, itself a country which unites its people by adhering to strong ideological principles, this shock has been difficult to absorb, and the shock-waves have reverberated. The loss of ideological unity in the former Soviet Union may have increased stress on the USA's own faltering ideological unity, paving the way for potential political fragmentation.

As we have seen, in order to promote cohesion and a sense of national identity, the United States has, since its formation, 'created' its *raison d'être* from its founding documents: the Declaration of Independence and the Constitution. The first lesson learned by millions of US school children has been that 'We the people . . .' draughted the Constitution, and that government was created '. . . of the people, by the people, for the people'. Unlike the UK, where authority is derived from the Monarch and Parliament, in the USA, authority – at least in popular perception – is derived from the people. Hence, the conceptualisation of 'the people' in political culture has long been of paramount importance. Lacking either the shared history and traditions of the nations of Western Europe, or the traditional linguistic dualism and multiculturalism of Canada (although that has provided only limited cohesion, as we shall see), the USA has historically promoted itself as a society where people discarded their ethnic identity to become 'Americans'.

This did not mean that America was ever the 'melting pot' envisaged by Emerson: a crucible where ethnic identities were melted down to form a new 'American' race comprised of the characteristics of the old ethnic identities in exact proportion to each other.[15] It meant, however, that those idiosyncrasies which immigrants did retain, at least temporarily, were, for the most part, manifested only in the private sphere, and that in matters of public life all people considered themselves firstly as Americans. John Quincy Adams summed up the mood when meeting a potential German emigrant: '[Immigrants] must cast off their European skin, never to resume it. They must look forward to their posterity rather than backward to their ancestors . . .'.[16]

The willingness of immigrants to 'cast off their European skin' correlated closely with their commitment to the democratic ideals expressed in the Constitution. Writing in 1831, the French writer Alexis de Tocqueville praised American society, commenting that the key to its unity was the participation of its people in civic life.[17] De Tocqueville also observed a less praiseworthy trend: in observing slavery he noted that racism was inherent in US society.[18] By this analysis, blacks, having been oppressed in slavery for nearly all of the first century of America's existence and even after the Reconstruction Amendments, and having been virtually excluded from participating in civic life (in some areas until the passage of the Civil Rights legislation in the early 1960s), could hardly be expected to take on the same 'American' identity as whites. The accordance of civil rights could not undo more than two centuries of racism.

Of course, other ethnic groups have also been marginalised in American society. The 'melting pot' only operated selectively. The Irish and the Germans, for example, were castigated as 'undesirables', especially in Puritan New England. 'Nativism', which briefly held sway in the 1850s, found a political home in the 'Know-Nothing' party which campaigned for immigrants to be excluded from political participation.[19] The movement was absorbed, however, by the Civil War and the focusing of national attention on Westward expansion.[20] The massive influx of 27 million immigrants from Eastern Europe which began after the Civil War and continued into the early years of the twentieth century, also integrated uneasily into the dominant Anglocentric culture. Problems of resentment against immigrants known as 'hyphenated' Americans – Hungarian-American, Czech-American, Russo-American – were masked, just as 'Nativism' had been disguised half a century earlier, by the onset of war.[21] It was not uncommon for President Woodrow Wilson's public speeches in the early days of World War I to be pleas for people to 'become *thorough* Americans'.[22] As well as blacks, immigrants of South-East Asian origin were deliberately and explicitly denied the rights of full political participation, and the Chinese were either deported or banned from entering the United States under the so-called 1907 'Gentleman's Agreement' with China.[23] Nearly half a century later, Japanese immigrants were interned in prison camps during World War II.[24] Xenophobia was especially evident in public life, however, in the 1920s, and articulated in the 1924 Immigration Act, a law which set quotas for immigrants on the basis of national origin. It was an effort to preserve the racial composition of America as it had been in the late nineteenth century.[25]

Prejudice, however, did not extend to prohibiting those immigrants from Eastern Europe who *did* manage to enter the United States from taking up their rights as citizens of that country. Ironically, with employment, free public education and limited access to the vote, as well as other pressures on society such as the Great Depression, World War II and then the Cold War, immigrants eventually became stronger adherents to the American 'Creed' of liberty and democracy than many native-born Americans.[26]

As many racial issues were re-evaluated after the Civil Rights Movement, a new way of historical thinking became common.[27] There was a movement for minority groups to compensate for their historical losses through discrimination by re-interpreting the history of the United States in a way that enhanced the standing of their particular group. Minority groups, particularly blacks, recognise that the failure to celebrate the past is a reason for low self-esteem in the present, and seek to educate their people as to the part they have played in American history.

One such example may be the interest in recent years in the black regiments of the Union Army in the Civil War. To give an example, the film *Glory* is dedicated to the 186,000 black soldiers who fought in that war.[28] The political significance of this is immense: history is a powerful weapon. 'The thing that has kept most of us, that is, African-Americans, almost crippled in this society, has been our complete lack of knowledge concerning the past', wrote Malcolm X.[29] The historian Michael Stumer explains this point:

> Loss of orientation and the search for identity are brothers . . . Anyone who believes that this has no effect on politics and the future ignores the fact that in a land without history, he who fills the memory, defines the concepts, and interprets the past, wins the future.[30]

The trend to eliminate the traditional 'Anglocentric' domination of education, and hence 'Anglocentric' political life has both positive and negative implications for the unity and stability of the USA.

Re-interpretation of history is valuable as a means of raising black self-esteem and helping blacks to become participants in the American polity. It is, however, a force for instability when educators believe that black children learn better when separated from white children and following a different curriculum.[31] This 'new' separatism is in vogue with many black (and white) educators: campuses are fragmented, many have black dormitories, black common-rooms, black tables in dining halls. Moreover, there is an influential school of thought which argues that black students only learn if taught by black teachers, in the same way that, it is argued, feminist studies can only be taught by women. There are two possible corollaries to this trend, according to Schlesinger.[32] One is that only black people should do black studies, and only women can really understand feminism. The other is that, if only blacks can teach black history, then presumably only Italians, Poles and Irish can teach *their* history.

The combination of this school of thought with the existence of a large and rapidly increasing Hispanic population in the USA may also have implications for political stability. Already there are demands that Hispanic children be taught *only* in Spanish.

Harm [is not] done when ethnic groups display pride in their historic past or in their contributions to the American present. But the division of society into fixed ethnicities nourishes a culture of victimisation and a contagion of inflammable sensitivities.[33]

There is, therefore, a cultural attack on traditional 'American' identity as a 'common' identity for all US citizens.

The adherents to these educational philosophies are, however, in the minority and constitutionally-approved political separatism from blacks (or any other ethnic group) is unlikely at present. In order to avoid overstating such trends, it is important to note that there are also signs of increasing integration between ethnic communities. For example, in 1990 there were one million black–white marriages, compared to 310,000 in 1970.[34] Cultural trends are similar: in a popular Hispanic magazine, a readership survey revealed that the three most popular role models of Hispanic-Americans were all 'Anglo-Americans': Washington, Lincoln and Theodore Roosevelt.[35] There seems, therefore, to be a complex pattern of development in the growth of ethnic separatism and its interaction with cultural forces promoting integration into a common 'American' identity, an issue to which we shall return later in this chapter.

Concurrent with the fragmentation of the 'American' cultural ideology of 'nationhood' is evidence of a breaking down of the ideological differences which have been commonly perceived to distinguish the USA from Canada. Since 1965, Lipset's famous article 'Revolution and Counter-Revolution – The United States and Canada' has represented the orthodox view in comparative US and Canadian sociology.[36] Lipset refuted the assertion of Louis Hartz that colonial societies were made up of 'fragments' of the European 'home' countries of immigrants. Hartz argued that only a 'fragment' of the values, experiences and ideas of Europe were entrenched in North America because immigrants were almost wholly members of the working classes and, therefore, the conservatism of the upper classes did not become part of mainstream ideology.[37] Lipset, however, argued that the 'fragment' was less influential in the forming of American liberal democracy than the American Revolution itself. He stressed the 'revolutionary' aspect of the American Revolution, and the simultaneous emergence of universalistic and egalitarian ideology, to explain what he perceived to be the persistence of these values in contemporary US society. In contrast, Lipset characterised Canada as a 'counter-revolutionary' society, one which had absorbed the Empire Loyalists in 1776, and continued to define itself in opposition to the USA, long retaining a loyalty to the British Crown and an at once more hierarchical and more collectivist society.

In recent years, the 'revolutionary:counter-revolutionary' thesis has been challenged. Finbow, for example, argues that the ideological differences between the two countries are not derived from their 'organising principles', but rather from the way in which the two countries have been constrained by their different institutions to respond to similar pressures in society in dissimilar fashions.[38] Actual and proposed constitutional changes in Canada since 1982 have the potential to reshape Canadian political institutions to make them more like those of the USA.[39] Finbow suggests that the new authority of the judicial branch, for example, or the weakening of Parliamentary power (particularly if a more powerful, so-called 'Triple E', Senate is put in place which might then restrain activity in the House of Commons) will cause policy decisions to be made which reflect little or no ideological difference between Canada and the USA. According to this argument, further decentralisation in Canada – which seems an inevitability if the present stalemate is to be overcome – will, therefore, promote ideological convergence between the two countries.

Despite this perceived splintering of 'national' ideology, constitutional institutions in Canada have not yet changed to reflect this. The

'Triple E' Senate is still an unrealised aim of the Western provinces, and meaningful 'distinct society' status, let alone any sort of sovereignty, for Quebec is still to come about.

Encouraged by the traditional view of itself as a pluralistic society, without the American imperative for integrationist processes, Canada has sought to deflect pressures towards fragmentation by an inclusive approach. Rather than stressing the need for assimilation, the Canadian polity in 1982 included in its Constitution the rights of minority and ethnic groups to be 'different'. In this way, the Mulroney government hoped to absorb and diffuse the grievances of these groups.

The significance of such recently-created constitutional differences between the two countries can be seen clearly in the issue of women's rights. Since 1924, American feminist groups have consistently campaigned for the United States' Bill of Rights to be amended so as to include a clause protecting the rights of women.[40] Following the rise of the 'feminist wave' in the 1960s, and the foundation of the National Organisation of Women (NOW) in 1966, by 1972 the campaign had gained enough support to have the women's rights clause, the 'Equal Rights Amendment' (ERA), ratified by both the Senate and the House of Representatives, with 30 of the necessary 38 states ratifying in the first two years.[41] During the state ratification period of the next ten years, however, the feminist movement found that it could not apply the pressure necessary to obtain ratification in the remaining states.[42] Neither could it prevent internal division, caused particularly by the refusal to reach a consensus, lack of financial resources, poor campaign techniques, and pressures from the 'New Right' political philosophy – now all-powerful in American civic life. By June 1982, when the ratification period expired, the ERA was still unratified.[43]

By contrast, April 1982 saw the entrenchment in the Canadian Charter of Rights and Freedoms of Section 15, a gender equality clause.[44] This success of the feminist movement, however, must be linked to the fact that the federal government's attentions, at this time, were focused primarily on making Quebec a signatory to the Constitution. Had the gender-equality clause been an isolated demand, made in a time of general constitutional stability, then, perhaps, it would not have been ratified.

It is worth noting at this juncture that the feminist movement (apart from its extreme radical wing) was, and is, necessarily integrationist, rather than separatist. This means that feminist groups do not have the political leverage which was afforded to the black movement by its 'Black Nationalist' element. Consequently, political and constitutional gains are more difficult to achieve. Nevertheless, where the longer established American feminist movement was refused a place in the Constitution, and remains angry and embittered, the Canadian movement, although younger, was granted its demands. As a result, the women's movement has gained a place in the Canadian polity, where it has been able to advance its own agenda without threatening general political stability.

That Canada is, however, displaying signs of constitutional disintegration less than 130 years after Confederation is, perhaps, indicative of fatal flaws in the Constitution itself.[45] It may not be wholly due to significant demographic shifts or other structural changes in the Canadian state (although in 1986 newly-arrived immigrants made up 15.6 per cent of the population).[46] Despite the increasing multiculturalism of its population, linguistically Canada remains a state with a significant francophone minority (24 per cent) co-existing with the anglophone majority (61 per cent).[47] The fact that 21 per cent of this francophone minority is historically concentrated in Quebec means that this province has a francophone majority of 81.4 per cent.[48] So, pressures from Quebec have always lain heavily on the constitutional agenda, in a way not seen among any single group in the USA.[49]

The difficulties involved in managing Quebec's demands for 'distinct society' status have their roots in the way the Quebec francophones, the Québécois, were first absorbed into the Canadian state. When the British conquest of 'New France' was completed in 1759, the incorporation of an already established population was achieved through the 1763 Royal Proclamation. This demanded assimilation and allegiance to the British Crown and to Protestantism.

Ironically, however, pressures deriving from what was to become the USA halted the smooth development of a culturally and linguistically homogenous Canadian state. Prior hints of the ensuing rebellion in the 13 Colonies to the South made it expedient for Britain to preserve the separate identity of Quebec as a means of preventing Québécois participation in the rebellion. Hence, a significant precedent was created, the 1774 Quebec Act, which allowed the preservation of the French language, so-called 'feudal' system, Roman Catholicism (along with denominational education) and a civil code. From Canada's beginnings, therefore, Quebec saw itself as more than simply a constituent part of a greater body; it saw itself as a 'distinct society': a classic example of the enduring importance of the circumstances of state-formation, a point to which we will return in Chapter 4. The separatism of Quebec was effectively institutionalised in the Canadian state by the 1774 Act.

Seeking stability in North America, it was not until the late 1830s that Britain could afford to make another attempt at francophone assimilation. The British Crown divided Quebec along linguistic lines into (English) 'Upper Canada' and (French) 'Lower Canada'. It gave both colonies an equal distribution of powers (despite the greater population density in Lower Canada). This was intended to 'contain' francophone demands. Simultaneously, however, the arrangement gave the Québécois greater political autonomy, and an actually advantageous position when relative numbers of francophones fell because of steady anglophone immigration to Upper Canada.[50] Likewise, the formation of a Confederation of Canada in 1867, although it made francophones a much smaller minority in the Canadian entity, also allowed Quebec a further degree of autonomy. Quebec's nationalistic demands were preserved, finding expression both economically and politically.

Contemporary Canada faces specific requests for constitutional change from aboriginals and the West as well as Quebec. Yet, when the Constitution was patriated from Great Britain, by means of an amending formula, in 1982, only the nationalist *Parti Québécois* government of Quebec was sufficiently mobilised to articulate its ambitions.[51] The impetus for this came from the fact that the initial draft of the 1982 Act did not give Quebec a veto over Constitutional amendments. Moreover, the Quebec government was angered by the fact that the federal government was due to ratify a constitutionally entrenched Charter of Rights and Freedoms without the acquiescence of the Quebec legislature. The Charter was intended to protect individuals, not groups, rather in the manner of the United States' Bill of Rights. It also recognised the multicultural character of Canadian society, which was a potential threat to Quebec's distinctiveness.[52] Thus, in 1982, Quebec alone refused to sign the Constitution Act, and created the present stalemate, where Quebec is bound to a Constitution to which it is not a party.[53]

Demands from aboriginal peoples present another potential fissure in Canada. Territorially located, for the most part, in the far North, these peoples have been ignored for much of Canada's history.[54] The contemporary importance of the Yukon and Northwestern Territories as holders of precious natural resources gives aboriginals significant political leverage in Ottawa, and aboriginal demands for self-government are loud and articulate.

After the agreement, in the failed Charlottetown Consensus, to give aboriginal peoples self-government by 2002, it seems possible that they might eventually be successful. If so, this will cause still greater subdivision and divided sovereignty within Canada. Complicating matters further is the existence of aboriginal groups outside the North of Canada, which have, in the last two decades, become increasingly politically active and demanding of self-government and other traditional rights. Since the Territories do not have provincial status, greater political autonomy, with strong economic ties to the rest of Canada, is not perceived by the federal government to be a threat to federalism.[55]

Aboriginal demands for autonomy impinge on the future of the Northern-most American state, Alaska. This is a potential point of convergence between the USA and Canada. In 1867 its purchase from Russia hastened pressures in Canada for a Canadian Confederation.[56] Even now, on the one hand, the USA might find its ownership of Alaska (population 0.57 million) difficult if a strong movement for political separatism were to emerge in the Canadian West. On the other hand, however, as the importance of Alaska as a repository of economically invaluable natural resources eventually declines, its high population of 'Native Americans' might well be attracted by the self-government of its Canadian aboriginal neighbours, assuming that is achieved.

There are other emergent points of potential fissure in Canada which have often been masked by the highly visible political pressures from aboriginals and the Québécois. The federal system does not give equal representation and equal responsibilities to each province. The seats in the Canadian Senate are divided equally between four units: Ontario, Quebec, the Western provinces and the Maritime provinces. Western alienation has been a traditional theme in Canadian politics since Macdonald allocated federal money to the building of the Canadian Pacific Railway in the early years of Confederation.[57] The fear then was that Western Canada would so lag behind Central Canada in terms of economic expansion that it would be absorbed into the United States.[58] By 1992, however, the Western provinces constituted an economic unit large enough to challenge the federal government to substantially increase Western Senate representation, on an individual state basis, putting it on a par with that of Ontario and Quebec. This comprises merely the first of the West's demands for a so-called 'Triple E' (Equal, Effective, Elected) Senate. These demands have put pressure on the West's relationship with Quebec, such that in 1992, when the Charlottetown Accords seemed likely to let Quebec achieve 'distinct society' status, a significant proportion of Westerners claimed that they would not be unhappy to see Quebec leave Canada.[59]

It is, therefore, possible to observe a growing convergence between the USA and Canada, and this will be discussed later in this work. It is also possible to note that strong pressures towards political separatism and fragmentation exist in Canada, and may produce autonomous or semi-autonomous zones within what is now the Canadian state by the middle of the twenty-first century. This must renew interest in the trends to political separatism observed in the USA, and raises the question of whether potential fissures are visible in US politics.

Potential regional fissures are probably deeper beneath the surface in the USA than might at first appear, and may serve to override integrationist factors, at least in the political sphere. The South's tradition of 'state autonomy', which has been nurtured since the late 1960s by a successful Republican coalition, appears to have been submerged by the Democratic sweep of the Southern states in the 1992 Presidential election. Moreover, the shift of industrial, technological and economic power, from the Mid-West and New England, to the Southern 'Sunbelt', in recent years means that the economic disparities which aggravated the trend to autonomy are less evident.

Changes in the shape of the US economy alter employment opportunities and migration patterns.[60] New use of resources, innovation in technology and new methods of business organisation have had differing impacts across the USA and Canada, according to variation in regional constraints and contradictions. Economic reorganisation intensified after World War II, when there was a conscious shift away from the agricultural and manufacturing sectors of industry. Several large corporations began to out-run their nearest competitors and diversify their services (so becoming oligopolies) and these and other large corporations internationalised trade in the search for new markets. The most obvious spatial consequence of this reorganisation was decentralisation, initially from metropolitan areas to suburbs and then rural locations, where land was more readily available at less expensive prices.

Regional variation became more acute as large corporations, responding to economic pressure, both domestic and international, reorganised again. 'Branch plants' now carried out routine and standardised processes and the responsibility for more complex planning and research was taken back to a metropolitan centre, perhaps even on the other side of the country. The Southern and Western states of the United States gained, therefore, as production and production service jobs have been lost from the traditional Northern and Eastern 'Manufacturing Belt'.

Moreover, groups with diverse political agendas are emerging in this region. As a result of more successful litigation against discriminatory laws and electoral gerrymandering, blacks started to move back to the South in significant numbers from the 1970s onwards. Once in the

South, they moved to the cities, rather than rural areas, and were able to be more politically active. The South, especially Florida, has also seen a large increase in Hispanics: to give an example, Cuban immigrants make up over 60 per cent of the population of Miami.[61]

The dynamic of black poverty highlights an increasing polarisation between cultural groups and between rich and poor in American society.[62] Rich and poor are geographically, as well as socially, separated, the poor becoming entrenched in inner-city ghettos out of which there appears to be no escape route, while the middle-class rapidly relocate to the suburbs.[63] In the cities, community breakdown has accelerated in recent years; the 1992 Los Angeles riots are adequate evidence of what is demonstrably a more widespread process.

A significant convergence is also occurring between the economies of the United States and Canada, as well as in political affairs, while a similar trend links the US economy and that of Mexico. The foundation for this has already been laid. The Canada–United States Free Trade Agreement (FTA) of 1989 officially removed tariff barriers between the two states, an agreement which, significantly, received the most enthusiastic support from the Canadian provinces of Quebec and Alberta, where separatist tendencies are strongest.

In November 1993 the North American Free Trade Agreement (NAFTA) was ratified in the United States Congress, bringing Mexico into this free trade zone. From 1 January 1994, therefore, the FTA has been subsumed into NAFTA. NAFTA does not anticipate political integration between its members; the key points of the Agreement are of an economic nature. All goods deemed by the adjudicator to have significant 'North American' content may be moved freely between the member states. (There are some special provisions for agricultural goods such as sugar, orange juice and maize.)[64] It attempts a degree of harmonisation on environmental and labour force policies. A Commission for Environmental Co-operation (CEC) has been set up to ensure the members comply with their national environmental law, although as yet this body has limited enforcement powers. It can only impose a maximum fine of $20 million on miscreants, and does not, for example, have a mandate to examine the use or misuse of natural resources.[65]

Effectively, trade barriers between Canada and Mexico have also been removed, a development which few had considered seriously when Canada had begun talks with the United States on free trade less than a decade previously. Indeed, there is substantial opposition to NAFTA in Canada from people who consider themselves forced into a free trade agreement with Mexico, a country Canada has had little trade with in the past. Canadian jobs, it is feared, will be lost to Mexico, where labour costs are lower. Admittedly, Canada, with its economy more focused on the processing of raw materials, has greater cause to worry on this matter than the United States.

Nevertheless, more than two years after NAFTA was first put in place, there is scant evidence of the Agreement making a negative impact on Canadian jobs. More often, Canadian criticism of NAFTA comes from those who see it as a vehicle for US 'cultural imperialism'. Anxious to guard against this criticism, the drafters of the NAFTA bill inserted a provisionary clause which means that the cultural industries of Canada are not subject to the general rules on services.[66] Although this clause has reduced antipathy towards NAFTA in Canada, it has not been entirely successful. In early 1995, for example, some American television stations refused to play Canadian videos on air in protest against Canada's insistence that Canadian advertising in an American magazine did not constitute a 'Canadian cultural product', and, therefore, could not be freely imported into Canada.[67] Some sectors of the population in the USA, and indeed in Canada, perceive this to be Canadian cultural protectionism.

Whether or not US cultural imports are controlled, the cultural convergence of the USA and Canada is already fast advancing. There is also long-standing cultural convergence along the Northern border of the USA. Most of Canada's population is concentrated along this relatively narrow strip of land, reflecting that country's asymmetrical relationship with the USA throughout its history. Canada's diet of American cultural exports grows rapidly as media technology improves. While the fact that the border has survived for more than a century may lend credence to the idea that forces for convergence are not strong, as Southern USA becomes increasingly multicultural, particularly Hispanicised, this may enhance the common Western European Protestant culture of Northern Americans and a majority of Canadians, so forming a new cultural zone across existing national borders.

Another significant potential consequence of NAFTA is an acceleration of the trend towards economic convergence between neighbouring Canadian and US regions. The Western Canadian provinces and the Northwestern American states have rapidly growing economies, with several points of similarity; they already operate long-standing agreements on the sharing of off-shore resources. Moreover, both regions are geographically alienated from their political capitals, Washington DC, and Ottawa. Similarly, if the New England states and the Maritime provinces were to maximise the commonalties in their economies, then these regions might also converge (as some early nineteenth-century Canadian colonists feared they might do). The economic pressures here would, however, have to outweigh the subsidies the Maritimes currently receive from the Canadian federal government. If they continue, or become more exaggerated – as suggested above – this combination of cultural and economic pressures may erode the present differences between US citizens and Canadians during the next half-century.

Similar factors may be at work in the South of the USA, where US cultural imports also flow freely across the border, as illustrated by migrants bringing Hispanic culture to the USA. The incorporation of Mexico in the free trade zone may anticipate greater Central American–South Western USA convergence.[68] Proponents of NAFTA in both Mexico and the United States argued that it would enlarge the economies of both countries, while anti-NAFTA forces in the USA pointed out that the Mexican economy, stimulated by large imports of American goods and services, would grow more rapidly than that of the USA.

The US International Trade Commission predicted increased economic convergence as Mexican exports to the USA increased in certain sectors of trade and American exports were reciprocated in other sectors.[69] There has commonly been anticipated a temporary flow of labour-intensive jobs from the USA to Mexico while Mexican labour remains cheaper and the economy smaller.

Economic convergence may even precipitate political convergence. Indeed, Mexico, after traditionally shunning economic links with the United States – to the extent of refusing to join GATT in the early 1980s – initiated negotiations for NAFTA in 1990. This was a result of increased governmental communication and co-operation between the two countries.

Political co-operation is particularly necessary with regard to the United States–Mexican border, stretching for 3,234 km and notoriously difficult to police. Illegal entry into the United States has increased rapidly since the 1960s. In 1993 President Clinton made $172.5 million available for anti-illegal immigration measures, most of which were aimed at curbing the flow of Hispanics over the Southern border with Mexico.[70] It is doubtful that this in itself will reduce illegal immigration from Mexico, estimated at more than 30,000 people a year in 1993.

It is, perhaps, more likely that one of the consequences of NAFTA will be the eventual stabilisation of migration patterns from Mexico to North America, as it becomes less economically advantageous to move to the USA. In the short term, however, both legal and illegal immigration may increase, as Mexicans are both 'pushed' by competition for jobs at home (the population of Mexico, 85 million in 1993, is estimated to rise to 136 million by 2025[71]) and 'pulled' by better jobs in the South Western USA.

Whether immigration from Mexico increases or decreases, the USA still has to adjust to the implications of a greater Hispanic content in its population mix than prior to the 1980s. The 1990 Census revealed that California (the most populous state with 30.38 million inhabitants), New Mexico and Texas had populations which were more than 20 per cent Hispanic, while Arizona, Colorado and New York's populations were between 10 and 20 per cent Hispanic.

Using this data, the Bureau of the Census estimated that by 2080 Hispanics would constitute 23.4 per cent of the United States population, with a significant concentration in the South West. As part of the cultural pluralist trend in US society, and despite some acculturation into US political culture, Hispanics often retain political values relating to a tradition of 'absolutism' and, therefore, do not adjust quickly to American liberal democracy.[72] The Cuban exile population, for example, has mainly anti-Marxist ideals and tends to look for political models to the more strongly anti-Marxist states of South America, although it remains to be seen whether this will continue after the demise of Castro.

As yet, Hispanic groups do not form more than significant state minorities; neither do they wield enough political or economic power to present a threat to the political stability of the USA. Indeed, although California's economy is one of the healthiest in the United States, California's Hispanic and black populations remain among the most disadvantaged groups in society.[73] Nevertheless, the rapid expansion of the United States' Hispanic population might well be seen as a foundation for either separatism or a potential political convergence between Central America and the (Hispanic) South West of the United States. The very disadvantages of this section of the population in US society may serve to politicise it, as occurred with the black community.

Other pressures on North America derive from Latin America. Since the early nineteenth century, the United States has regarded this region as a strategic part of its security arrangements. The 'Monroe Doctrine' of 1823 attempted to forbid the rest of the world, particularly the European powers, from interfering in Latin America: ' . . . the American continents . . . are henceforth not to be considered as subjects for colonisation by any European powers'.[74] Yet, although anxious to prevent outside interference in Latin America, North America was hesitant about using its own influence there, concentrating instead on Westward expansion as a means to secure itself as a stable, industrial, nation-state. After World War II, however, United States hegemony escalated both economically and culturally.

In 1947 the USA initiated and signed the Inter-American Treaty of Reciprocal Assistance, and in 1948 established the Economic Commission for Latin America.[75] Throughout the ensuing Cold War period, it maintained this attitude, especially in the face of Marxist influences, perceived by the US administration to be threatening. The events leading up to the Cuban Missile Crisis of 1962 and Reagan's persistent attempts to overthrow the Sandinistas in Nicaragua are but two demonstrations of the desire of American governments to make Latin American politics congruent with their own.[76]

In the post-Cold War era, however, the US government has perceived that it no longer needs to keep itself so politically and economically engaged in South America.[77] It has adopted a slightly more relaxed attitude to international 'rules', and consequently made priorities of such issues as tariffs, subsidies, countervailing duties and commodity transfers. These all constitute potential sources of instability in future North American–Latin American relations. Simultaneously, several Latin American states are no longer so dependent on North America, and the relative economic position of North America has declined.

The 1980s transformation of America from a creditor into a debtor nation under the policy of 'Reaganomics' may eventually release Latin American states from dependence on the American economy. Nevertheless, in the short term, Latin American states are hampered by the decline of the United States' economy, since this reduces aid and imports.[78]

Dependence on the USA in other spheres is also less certain. For instance, contemporary Central and South America display evidence of modern European cultural and political influences as well as those from the USA.[79] With the collapse of the Soviet Union many Latin American political groups which had political allies in the Soviet Union were forced to seek new partners, for example, by forging links with the social democratic parties of Western Europe.[80]

As a result, the rise of the European Union as a major economic bloc, coupled with the end of the Cold War, has resulted in the USA becoming both politically disengaged in Latin America and potentially culturally and economically challenged in the region by the European interests. Interestingly, a similar loosening of dependence on the USA can be seen in Europe itself, where NATO no longer has to depend upon American military might for its security, while the relative economic positions of the United States and Germany have changed drastically since the establishment of the post-Cold War order.[81]

Consequently, as the relationship of dependence which kept US troops in Europe after World War II is challenged within both the USA and the EU, so the US engagement with Latin American politics is declining in significance.[82] Such changes are inevitably weakening the place of the USA in the NATO command structure in *de facto* rather than *de jure* terms, and in Europe overall, in addition to lessening its importance in the Americas.[83] In economic terms, 'trade war' between the USA and Europe is merely a possible outcome of a divergence of interests in a climate of economic stress.[84] So, the changed military and economic relationships in Europe, and between Europe and the USA, impact upon both US security and on the role of the USA in the security of the American continent.

The expected 'peace dividend' (potentially stimulating economic growth and enhancing government spending) has not, therefore, strengthened either the US economy or its role in international politics; rather it has resulted in the ability of the EU to take a dominant role in European politics and economics and of Latin America to become less dependent on US security and economic interests.[85] While the end of the Cold War enabled a brief illusion in the USA of a monopolar world of unrivalled US global dominance,[86] within the Americas the end of an emphasis on ideological unity brought about by the cessation of the Cold War has promoted a greater move to political and economic independence in Latin America alongside economic and cultural convergence in North America and between the USA and Mexico.

These changes have also made domestic consensus on foreign policy matters very difficult to achieve, itself rendering rapid deliberate action (for example, in Bosnia) hard to accomplish.[87] If the pressures from within US politics are partly towards securing the continuing international role of the country, there are also significant factions in government and the military pressing for major disengagement from European security in a more formal fashion.[88] Again, the internal divisions within the United States are subtle and seemingly contradictory, but the pattern is one of internal loss of consensus and external retraction.

The implications of the new relationship between Latin America and the USA are also uncertain. South and Central America, with the booming population of economically 'deprived' but active adults, seems an immense reservoir of potential migrants. If large numbers of Central American Hispanics were to move north into the South Western USA, then the vacuum left in the Central American workforce would probably be filled by a movement of population from South America, or possibly even by immigrants from outside the Americas. The result of such a mass-migration on the domestic stability of the USA can only be guessed at. If no such movement occurs, then the internal pressures brought about by increased population pressure in South and Central America might be seen as a major destabilising factor in those regions, so impacting on the stability of the USA. So, the imbalance between North and South within the Americas already contains within it the potential for instability. It is a moot point whether the present situation is the 'lull before the storm' in the relationship, or whether current and future policies within the USA and in the South of the Americas will be able to contain this pressure, or channel it into (stable) expression.

TWO SPECIAL CASES: ALASKA AND HAWAII

The states of Alaska and Hawaii did not join the USA until 1959, and are the principal 'detached' territories of the American state. These two states present special problems for both cultural and economic reasons, which may leave their future in the USA uncertain.

Alaska[89]

Alaska is potentially a very wealthy state with considerable natural resources – especially oil – and a tourist trade capable of increased exploitation as flight-times and other factors present less of a problem for travellers. Under-populated in comparison with most US states, Alaska seems distant from the majority of Americans: 'the last frontier'. With a relatively large Native American population still resident in the state and a strong tradition of personal independence and individualism, separatism from the USA could find support if part of a process advanced in other areas, especially in the context of the fragmentation of Canada, with which Alaska shares a common border.

Economically, given trade with its neighbouring Canadian territories and the continued exploitation of the oil and tourist industries, Alaska could be a viable independent economic unit. The same is also true of Hawaii, where separatist pressures already exist and cultural differences from the majority of 'mainland' Americans are deep-seated.

Hawaii[90]

Unlike other American states, Hawaii has an economy essentially dependent on a single source of income: tourism. Tourism accounts for up to 60 per cent of Hawaii's economy, whether directly or indirectly, and is the mainstay of the island's prosperity. As a US state, it is unsurprising that this trade has concentrated on US tourists, but the numbers of these (and the propensity to make return visits) are declining. In 1992–93, for example, there was a 17 per cent fall-off in tourist numbers from the USA.

Hawaii has increasingly to seek an Asian–Pacific tourist market and this, along with its geographical position, is likely to draw it towards the Asian, rather than American, states if this trend continues. Moreover, the Hawaiian population contains a substantial indigenous element (approximately 20 per cent of the total) disaffected with the USA. This indigenous population sees its identity more in Pacific than in American terms, and has fared poorly from the US involvement in the island overall.

The government of the state of Hawaii is also a problem for the continued retention of the island in the USA. It is heavily dominated by corporate interests and virtually a monolithic Democrat administration. With the current senators ageing the potential for a fresh approach to government may present itself before the year 2000.

Finally, there is the pressure towards separatism felt from pressure groups themselves. Marginal at present, these could become a significant factor if economic collapse hardens the attitudes of the non-indigenous population towards the USA, in the face of intensified tourism from a newly-prosperous Asia. The cultural lure of the Pacific may be too much for the Hawaiian population, especially given that 45 per cent of its non-indigenous inhabitants are of Asian origin.

SOME IMPLICATIONS FOR THE USA

If current demographic trends continue, the USA will change fundamentally in cultural terms over the next half century. Estimates suggest that by 2050 Asian-Americans will outnumber Black-Americans, and the Hispanic-American population will outnumber the Black-American population by about the same time.[91] Black, Asian and Hispanic groups are, for the most part, very different in culture, history, values and outlook from the non-Hispanic European-Americans, once the bulk of the 'white' population.[92] Moreover, non-Hispanic European-Americans will drop from 75 per cent to 53 per cent of the population.[93] These changes will be more acute, regionally, as California, Texas and Florida have both the fastest-growing populations in the USA and the greatest number of Hispanic Americans, proportional to the rest of their populations.[94] Even in the mid-1980s, Hispanics made up 25–30 per cent of the Californian population, but among elementary schoolchildren – the adult US citizens of the year 2000 – this proportion was more than 50 per cent.[95]

The cultural implication of these changes is that approximately half of the US population in the mid twenty-first century will derive from groups culturally distanced from those currently dominant and it has been suggested by *The Economist*[96] that Asian- and Hispanic-Americans may prove to be less sympathetic to the Black-American social and economic inequalities than have non-Hispanic European-Americans.[97]

Many of the members of the Hispanic group are likely to retain Spanish as at least a second language, especially if single language teaching were to become widespread, while they may be expected to share greater sympathy with Latin America and, perhaps, less with non-Hispanic Europe.[98] The rise of a significant Asian section of the population may lead to a re-orientation of public perceptions of – and attitudes to – Asia itself, a response assisted by the new Asia–Pacific emphasis of the US economy.[99] In some areas, including those closest to the Latin American South, the cultural definition of US citizens and Mexicans may become very blurred, and legal and illegal population and economic flows across the south border of the USA increase.[100] As we have seen, a similar distinct regional culture may be produced by cultural convergence in the Northern USA with Canada. Again, economic factors may stimulate and assist each of these trends.

In terms of the effect on a black population finding itself still socially disadvantaged but now much more marginalised, this could be a disruptive situation.[101] Likewise, it is hard to credit that 'white extremists' will be willing to see such changes happen without violent response;[102] the emergence of distinctively Hispanic regions inside the USA could be a stimulus to such extremists.

These changes in North American culture may be enhanced by the rapid 'Protestantisation' of Roman Catholic Latin America observable in the present.[103] Protestantism, especially evangelical fundamentalism, has appealed to both Hispanic- and Asian-Americans and to the citizens of Central American states in recent years, resulting in remarkable changes in religious allegiance. Similar advances in the Asia–Pacific area (especially in South Korea but, to a lesser extent, in Taiwan and

Singapore) may promote such trends in a newly Asia-looking USA.[104]

It may not be an exaggeration to envisage a Protestant, Spanish-speaking (or Spanish:English bilingual) zone emerging in the Americas, sharing a common culture, from California to Brazil, regardless of national boundaries. It is not inconceivable that this could promote either separatist, or 'internationalist', trends in the Southwest and Southeast of the USA, but it is unlikely to lead to a lessening of other differences between this Hispanic area and the non-Hispanic zone adjacent to Canada, nor with the black community.

All of these patterns, it must be stressed, are already (arguably) emerging, and have been documented in other studies, although their significance and combined effects have appeared to have gone unnoticed. The localisation of the black population in the Southern states and in the East, outside of the most Hispanicised and Asian areas for the most part, may combine with these trends to lead to stronger regional cultural differences in the USA than are experienced at present, and these may be supported by both economic and separatist pressures.[105] Culturally, therefore, the principal factor leading to destabilisation is likely to be changes in the cultural identity of the majority of the population.

The potential of Hawaiian separatism in the US Pacific territories themselves is less clear, although this is already a somewhat culturally-distinct state. The ability of US Pacific islands to gain independence is already evidenced in the independence of the Marshall Islands in 1990, and of the Palau Islands in 1982, but it is unclear whether its status as a federal state will prevent this in the case of Hawaii.[106]

ECONOMIC PROBLEMS IN THE USA: THE PROBLEM OF PERMEABILITY

The multinational corporation came into its own after 1945, when US MNCs expanded the scope of their operations and grew in number.[107] Between the start of the 1950s and the late 1960s, the stereotypical MNC was US-owned, its profits swelling the US economy.

Such corporations eroded the mercantilist basis of economic affairs, increasing the permeability of national economies to the extent that these could be 'mined' by 'outside' corporations of this sort. Similar developments can be traced in multinational banking, closely connected with the rise of US MNCs, and both institutions operated within the Bretton Woods economic system, working to US advantage.[108]

While among the 'top ten' MNCs in 1995 the majority remain

American-owned, the increase in the number of non-US MNCs operating in the USA is a noticeable feature of the 1980s and 1990s.[109] This continues: in 1985, 46 per cent of headquarters of the top industrial companies were in the USA, but in 1989 this figure was only 33.4 per cent.[110] When this is combined with the observation that the Bretton Woods institutions have themselves run into problems and calls for reform, which may be underway, then the US-led MNC-based transnational economy of the 1950s and 1960s seems irreparably changing away from US economic interests.[111]

This pattern of US economic developments can also be traced in the shift in focus of multinational banking from the US to the Asia–Pacific region, accompanied by increased competition to US trade and industry from both Asia and Europe.[112] The result of this has, in part, been a loss of markets for US companies but, perhaps more significantly, a serious invasion of US markets by overseas competitors.[113] To give a single example, albeit an evocative one, the largest hamburger 'chain' in the USA is now UK-owned.[114]

The globalisation of international economies has, therefore, produced an intensified permeability in the US domestic market, which has reduced US-based MNCs' ability to lead the American economy, and the domestic economy's ability to increase in size to offset the intensification of overseas competition. This has to be set in the overall context of US economic problems, and the effects of NAFTA on the continental economy.

NAFTA AND US ECONOMIC PROBLEMS

If US trade and industry is suffering from increased non-American competition and outside investment in the US economy, the effects of NAFTA are hardly likely to reduce this.[115] The formation of a continental market is, arguably, to the advantage of US companies within the Americas, but it also increases the trend towards permeability.[116]

The results of economic interaction with the USA's neighbours are already being felt. Following a detailed survey of US:Mexican economic relations in 1991 (before NAFTA) it was already noticeable that 'the evolution of their respective policies has made Mexico and the United States increasingly dependent on each other' and one might note the intensity of US:Canadian economic interactions also.[117] Yet, we have noted that this new 'interdependence' is not the same thing as Cold War economic and security 'dependency' – it is not a 'one-way' process of US leadership or domination in Mexican and Canadian markets.

As another survey undertaken in 1991 concluded: 'the economic attractions are sufficiently strong to make a coherent North American Economic Alliance an odds-on favourite by the end of the century'.[118] Such an erosion of national economic frontiers, combined with increased permeability to foreign MNCs, is liable to prove a hindrance rather than a stimulus to the USA's ability to rely upon its internal market in times of global economic stress. The USA is now 'locked into' the continental economy but not in such a way as to make this economy a resource-pool upon which the USA can draw at will. The combination of these factors has serious implications for the future of the US domestic economy.

That is, if it was the huge internal market of the US which led to its economic success in the twentieth century, or the continental market afforded by the Americas, this is unlikely to survive as a source of national economic strength into the mid-twenty-first century. While the development of this continental free trade zone may promote growth in the international economy only if it is operable as a protected, neo-mercantilist, internal market, can it form an engine for economic growth in the USA?

The implications of protectionism are so severe for the US economy, especially *vis-à-vis* the Asian and EU blocs, that this would almost certainly itself lead to a dramatic decline of the role of the US in the international economy, with resulting domestic economic impacts. The withdrawal or limitation of foreign commercial activity or investment could also prove disastrous to the US economy.[119] So protectionism, attractive as it may be to isolationists in the US administration, is no solution to the economic problems which the USA faces.

The regional disparities visible in the US economy may also be a source of problems. If California retains a sufficient economic base to differentiate it from the East coast states and mid-West, and it orientates its trade increasingly towards the Asia–Pacific zone of economic growth, it may fare disproportionately well in contrast to the traditional industries and domestic or European orientation of other regions.[120] Likewise, a 'Southern States' economy strongly integrated with that of Latin America (through NAFTA) could have major socio-political implications alongside and within the trends already discussed. Economic convergence between the Northern USA and Canada, simultaneously with these trends, could produce economic forces literally pulling the US economy apart.

The most destabilising aspects of economic change in the USA may, however, be the direct effects on the most underprivileged groups in US society itself. This will form the next topic of analysis.

There seems to be general agreement among US and other econo-mists that the US economy is in dire straits. The current budget deficit is a major political and economic problem, and while it is declining in scale, the current deficit is one of the US government's major worries.[121]

There are outstanding economic commitments if the USA is to maintain its global role, especially with respect to military and aid spending. While military spending is being cut, this is at some cost to US military supremacy.[122] Consecutive cuts will certainly reduce the relative military strength of the USA *vis-à-vis* its allies and potential opponents, but this is not a major problem given its considerable lead in this area. It may, however, further reduce the ability of the USA to play a major role in Europe.

Much more worrying is the need to cut domestic welfare spending in the face of growing social problems. The Director of the Office of Management and Budget has estimated that current spending levels on welfare are going to be difficult to maintain.[123] By 2013 it will no longer be possible to maintain the social security system, and cuts already affect the most sensitive groups, as identified earlier in this chapter, in terms of state stability.[124]

Current proposals already include cutting welfare to legal immigrants and mothers under eighteen years old.[125] A five-year limit will be imposed on other welfare payments, and payment will no longer be linked to the birth-rate of those on welfare.[126] That is, the Hispanic and other immigrant groups who will increasingly (as we have seen) make up the urban poor in American cities, will have to subsist outside of the welfare system.[127]

This would be less worrying if these were not the same groups most affected by the downturn in the economy.[128] Unemployment is rising and for almost all American citizens (81 per cent or more) real wages have been dropping in the last decade.[129] The implication of these changes is that the poor are getting poorer, and the poor are getting less help from the state.[130]

The emergence of an alienated and impoverished 'underclass' in American cities is often the stuff of 'horror stories' told by political scientists and the media, yet it seems to be forming as the US economy slides into decline. This situation is aggravated by the cultural and linguistic tensions already examined, leading to the under-employment of Hispanics especially. Two further aggravating factors must also be taken into account.

GUN-OWNERSHIP AND THE RISE OF LAWLESSNESS

The USA has a very high level of private gun-ownership compared to Western Europe and Australasia. In 1993, 200 million private guns were in circulation, counting only legal weapons (among a population of 249.9 million people).[131] In a single year there were approximately 20,000 gun-related killings and the gun-ownership lobby is 18 million strong (to count only members of the national rifle association).[132] Weapons in circulation include both handguns and shotguns, but also military-style semi-automatic rifles.

The highly-armed US population has a significant problem in the rise of lawlessness, especially in the cities. Murder, drugs-related crime and violence all exceed levels in the majority of Europe and Australasia.[133] Such is the extent of the problem in some parts of the USA that law-abiding private citizens have sought measures for their own defence in the cities, using fences, guards and other means to build 'defensible space' within which they can live without fear of crime.[134]

Criminalisation of the alienated poor is especially rife in the cities, where discontent and inequalities of opportunity aggravate the situation. In a society in which armed violence and lawlessness have become 'normalised' into the everyday experience of the poor, this trend has a potentially explosive character.

SOCIAL POLARISATION AND INTER-COMMUNAL VIOLENCE

The growing distance in culture and income between rich and poor is aggravated by an increasing trend towards social and economic zonation in US cities, and even regions.[135] This involves the concentration of similar socio-economic groups in distinct areas, which can then become, by a commonly-perceived 'social geography', associated with class and ethnic divisions. A clear example is the contrasts visible in contemporary Los Angeles.[136]

Polarisation in job opportunities and, to some extent, in education also aggravates these distances between social groups. This trend is likely to become more, rather than less, pronounced if the situation in the cities does not improve in regard to lawlessness and violence.

The prospects for social harmony in a divided America in which the rich and poor share few common bonds of residence, culture, education or opportunity and in which they are employed in drastically different ways (if at all) are grave. This is a recipe for serious social unrest.

Yet the communities in the poorer sections of US society are also both disunited and frequently mutually antagonistic. While this makes all-out revolution very implausible, even if social deprivation increases to become even more acute, the breakdown of inter-communal relations seems already to be an advanced aspect of US society.

In Los Angeles, where racial tension led to the recent riots, there are also serious hostilities between the black and Asian communities,[137] and between these communities and the Hispanics. According to *The Economist*, 'many black Americans believe Asians are stealing their livelihoods' and Asian–American shops have already been burnt by black militants.[138] The magazine quotes one black militant leader as stating, 'Mexicans and Koreans don't deserve to work if we don't work'.[139] In a situation of aggravated poverty and increased unemployment this attitude could easily become far more prevalent.

INSTABILITY IN MODERN AMERICA

The results of this survey, when combined, make worrying reading. Increased regionalism and separatism, enhanced cultural differences and an erosion of US national identity, can all be paralleled in Canada. In the US, however, this is combined with fundamental demographic changes leading to major cultural upheavals, at a time of increasing social deprivation and alienation among the very groups most affected. Economic decline, but probably not economic collapse, is liable to enhance these characteristics, but the relationship may be two-way: a feedback effect into the US economy promoting further decline.

Lawlessness and a heavily armed populace with intercommunal violence is likely both to increase social and spatial polarisation between classes and to reduce the 'governability' of US cities. These trends may feed back into separatist, or at least politically independently-minded, groups, increasing the credibility and appeal of their claims.[140]

When combined with the attractions to cultural regions within the USA towards Latin America and Canada in social and economic terms, and fundamental regional cultural differences between communities inside the state, this could lead to an erosion of the territorial integrity of the USA. Once such a process is underway, Hawaii and Alaska must be among those territories most likely to secede.

Yet such dramatic processes of collapse do not seem at present to loom in the immediate future. Far more plausible in this century is the increase of tensions and conflicts leading to an internal dynamic of civil disorder and fragmentation in the USA. If this occurs, the 'US empire' will, indeed, be in relative decline. The key questions must be, how likely is it that these trends will continue, and how plausible is the concept of separatism in North America? These questions will form the basis of the next two chapters.

3 The Rise of Separatism in Canada

The culturally-based, regional separatist trend identifiable in the USA is more advanced in Canada for historical reasons. In Chapter 2 we saw some of the ways in which separatist groups have emerged in Canada during the 1980s and 1990s, and the increasing irrelevance of national boundaries to these trends.[1] In this chapter the most advanced of these separatist trends anywhere in North America will be examined in detail: the case of Quebec. Quebec was incorporated into the Canadian Confederation as an already politically and culturally distinct province, so it is unsurprising that its separatist movement is the most developed of its kind in North America.

As such, the analysis of the recent history of the Quebecois nationalist movement is of interest to the general questions addressed in this book for two reasons. First, it might serve as an analogy for the potential future development of regional separatism in North America in general. Second, it might have a major impact on the fortunes of regional separatism in the USA, in view of the convergence which we saw in the previous chapter between the Northern USA and Canada. In other areas of the world, limited success by one regional separatist movement has led to the rise of other regionalist groups, so a 'knock-on effect' is possible.

If Quebec was to become independent or become part of a looser confederation of Canada, then other Canadian regionalists may seize their opportunity to make equivalent demands. Of these, Native Canadians, or 'First Nations', have already obtained a degree of political autonomy within the Canadian state, as we saw in the preceding chapter.

The likelihood of a 'knock-on' effect in the USA is enhanced by convergent trends, whether social (through Americanisation and intense cultural exchanges) or economic, as promoted by NAFTA. The erosion of a strict delineation, in all but political terms, between Northern USA and Southern Canada might, as a result, be one of the most significant changes in the social and economic geography of North America. This is not to underplay those changes visible in the South and West of the USA. These are bringing about a similar erosion of differences with Latin America. Such changes stress the way in which a combination of factors are aggravating the problems for the continued political stability of the USA caused by the internal societal and economic crises in the USA itself, and are likely to play a far greater role in future in shaping the political history of the Americas than at present.

The following account will, therefore, examine the detailed history of the Québécois separatist movement in the 1980s and 1990s, showing how this has led, within an apparently stable unitary state, to a serious prospect of the political fragmentation of Canada. It will be seen that this has been achieved without violent revolutionary upheavals and in a gradual way, similar to that which may be seen as occurring in the USA.

In October 1992 Canadians were asked to approve an agreement made by the federal government, the provincial governments and aboriginal leaders, which would, if ratified, make all ten provinces signatories to the Constitution. The nation-wide referendum, however, returned an emphatic negative vote on the so-called Charlottetown Consensus on the Constitution. The Consensus was intended to balance the Quebec government's demands for 'distinct society' status and guaranteed representation in the House of Commons, against the desire of Western provincial governments for an equal, elected and effective Senate. It was also designed to recognise (for the first time) aboriginal demands for self-government. The rejection of the Consensus reflected Québécois concerns that the 'distinct society' clause was not strong enough, and the anger from the West at the weakness of the reforms for which it had lobbied. There was also a general dissatisfaction with the federal government and its track record of failed attempts at constitutional renewal.

For Quebec, the failure of the Charlottetown process facilitated two significant developments. Firstly, the province almost unanimously returned the separatist *Bloc Québécois* in the federal elections the following year. In September 1994, moreover, the province rejected its Liberal government and elected in its place the separatist *Parti Québécois* which promised to give the people of Quebec a referendum on sovereignty. This took place in October 1995, when the motion for independence tabled by the government was only narrowly rejected (by a margin of 1.2 per cent).

The attempt to find a constitutional settlement with which all people could align themselves has been continuing since 1934, when the federal government first sought to patriate the Canadian Constitution from the British Parliament at Westminster. Until recently, attempts revolved around the challenge of incorporating one francophone province (with a 'distinct society' view of devolution and autonomy) within a federation of nine anglophone provinces. The anglophone provinces all tend to favour strong centralist government. From 1934 to Pierre Trudeau's 'Victoria Charter' in 1971, regular efforts to find a satisfactory settlement were rejected by Quebec governments on the grounds that they did not protect Quebec as a 'distinct society'. Until 1980, attempts at constitutional change were laid aside.

Since 1980, two developments have occurred. These developments mean that, while it is now harder to reach a constitutional consensus, it is even more vital, for those who favour unity, to find one. The development which makes a constitutional consensus harder to reach is the increased political participation of people in the predominantly anglophone part of the country. While many people in Western provinces and aboriginal groups demand greater autonomy, they are joined to a pan-Canada group which, in the Constitution Act 1982, has a Constitution largely articulating only *their* vision of the federation. Furthermore, the attached Charter of Rights and Freedoms strengthens their group-rights and nurtures allegiance to the federal government. The Meech Lake Accord 1987 was yet another failed attempt to reach a constitutional agreement with Quebec. This time it attempted to bring Quebec into a Constitution which had been patriated and signed by the other nine provinces in 1982. This time it was not because governments disagreed, but because citizens articulated anger that the federal government was proceeding in a way incompatible with their ambitions. The foundations of Quebec nationalism were laid in the 1960s 'Quiet Revolution' in whose contemporary demands for 'distinct society' protection the majority of Québécois participate.

Where the issues once lay around accommodating one national minority and provincial majority into a federal system, they have broadened and now lie around addressing the demands of several national minorities. It is as these national minorities that the Québécois constitute a provincial majority.

A convenient starting point is the 1980 Quebec referendum on so-called 'sovereignty-association'. Nationalist fervour in Quebec had reached a peak in 1973 when 93 per cent of *Parti Québécois* supporters wanted independence for Quebec.[2] Until November 1976, however, it was not given democratic expression in the election of an *independentiste* government. In 1976 the *Parti Québécois* was voted into power in Quebec, taking a majority of seats in the so-called National Assembly. The new government promised 'expanded democracy', but it took until 1980 before constitutional issues could be addressed through a province-wide referendum. Instead, it passed the 1977 Charter of the French

Language (Bill 101), which attempted to reduce the use of English in Quebec by prohibiting the use of any language but French on public and commercial notices.[3]

In 1976 the federal government, under Trudeau, responded to the election of the *Parti Québécois* by commissioning the 'Task Force on Canadian Unity', which in due course recommended that:

> A new distribution of powers should, whenever it is desired or needed in order to fulfil the objectives of dualism and regionalism, recognise the distinctive status of any province or make it possible for a province to acquire such status.[4]

The federal government (before and after the report's publication) continued, however, to work at its own method of unity: bilingualism. This suggests a reluctance to examine Quebec's impetus for reform. It took the referendum of May 1980, with its unpredictable campaign and ultimate vote against sovereignty-association, to persuade the federal government that the people of Quebec, not merely political elites, were behind the demand for greater representation rights.

To see how this nationalist movement originated, it is necessary to look at the origins of the French presence in North America, for as we shall see in the next chapter the question of origins must lie at the heart of the analysis of trends in political change.[5] When the British conquered 'New France' in 1760, the people there, the *canadiens,* were already a settled and established population. In order to ensure their assimilation and allegiance to the British Crown and religion the British government issued the 1763 Royal Proclamation, but this soon had to be overlooked. There was, of course, a more immediate problem: the rebellion in the 13 Colonies to the south. As mentioned earlier, rather than have the *canadiens* of Quebec join the rebellion, the British government created a significant precedent, the Quebec Act 1774. The Act implicitly allowed the *canadiens* to retain their own language, and explicitly their feudal system, civil code, Roman Catholicism and denominational education. Hence, from Canada's origins Quebec saw itself as more than simply a constituent part of a greater body; it saw itself as a 'distinct society'.

By the late 1830s French-Canadian anger that this partnership was not being recognised resulted in nationalist rebellions by the *Patriotes* which forced Britain to respond. The response was to divide 'the Canadas' into (English) Upper Canada and (French) Lower Canada, giving each new colony equality in terms of representation, despite the fact that the French-Canadians were a demographically larger group than the English. Although intended to 'contain' the French, the arrangement in fact gave them greater autonomy and, when demographic trends changed, an advantage.[6] With this arrangement, called 'consociationalism' by some commentators,[7] which was characterised by elite accommodation, joint ministries, leadership coalition, double majorities and the rotation of the capital between Toronto and Quebec City, the *canadien,* or Québécois, sense of distinctness and partnership was nurtured rather than suppressed. So, distinctness was institutionally preserved.

Québécois aspirations were forced to go on the retreat as an overwhelming majority of anglophones joined the new federal state, formed by Confederation, or the British North America Act 1867. Significant responsibilities, including most economic controls, were relinquished to the federal government. Yet Section 93 of the Act gave the right of French language education for francophones outside Quebec where numbers warranted it. So, for Quebec, Confederation was not the 'containment' the 'Fathers of Confederation' intended it to be, but rather a focus for nurturing its cultural nationalism until it could be expressed economically and politically. At the heart of Canada, therefore, is a paradox: while one group sees federalism as a force for unity, the other sees it as a force for maintaining difference.[8]

The point at which contemporary Québécois nationalism emerged from federalism came in the 1960s. The 'Quiet Revolution', as it was called, has been widely interpreted.[9] At its simplest level it comprised the modernisation of Quebec society and the simultaneous growth of economic assurance among the Québécois. This new confidence then mobilised a renewed aspiration for Quebec to be an independent nation. This took the shape of a social transformation, which has been described in somewhat extreme terms as 'the most rapid industrial, social, educational and religious revolution in the Western world'.[10] While we would not necessarily agree with this characterisation, urbanisation *had* gradually brought about the demise of the rural parish, and hence the Roman Catholic Church in Quebec, a traditional controlling influence in social, health and educational institutions. The government moved in and filled the vacuum by a huge expansion of the state. As a result, this part of the economy became tied to government policy, through enterprise schemes and industrial planning. As the public sector grew, the personal economies of huge numbers of people became dependent on state expansion. In the space of ten years (1960–70) Quebec's public sector grew almost ten-fold, from 2 per cent to 15 per cent of the workforce.[11]

This process was, of course, being repeated in other provinces. Quebec was unique, however, in that it contained a francophone majority which had little economic interaction with the anglophone minority. Its private sector was controlled by anglophones and not open to francophones in a practical sense. The Quiet Revolution involved an ideological change and the economic transformation of a whole class; for as Lijphart observed,

> The angle at which religion and class cut across each other does not deviate much from a right angle, but the deviation that *is* present reflects the generally lower socio-economic status of (francophone) Roman Catholics.[12]

When expansion of the state took place, therefore, the people whose interests were mobilised were a highly specific group with a common cultural and historical identity. In this respect, rather than in the details of their history, they were similar to the groups today being mobilised inside the USA.

The 'new middle class' needed to sustain its status, and sought to do this by expanding its educational facilities.[13] As a result, the dynamics of the state expansion became self-perpetuating. Hundreds of young graduates were released into the workforce who, because of the closed nature of the private sector and the linguistic difficulties of working in other provinces, could only find work in the Quebec public sector.

By the mid-1970s the Québécois identity was caught up in the workings of the political state, only to find that the state had limited power. It was still bound by the constraints of working within the federal system; moreover, it was a federal system which – in the course of the last half century – had become set on a centralist track, due in part to the strength of original English-Canadian objectives. These were strong enough virtually to ignore several Royal Commissions and Reports which warned of the need to adjust the polity. Even in 1956, for example, the Royal Commission of Inquiry on Constitutional Problems had reported that:

> If Anglo-Canadian culture is today spread throughout nine of the ten provinces and if it can count upon their organised life for its diffusion and renewal, French-Canadian culture on the other hand has only one real focus, and that is the province of Quebec.

It then went on to stress the need for *mutual trust* if:

> as is its legitimate ambition, Canada should eventually give birth to an authentic 'nation' in whose midst the two groups will live in friendship, finding their full flowering . . .[14]

Yet the recommendations of this report and subsequent ones were greeted with intransigence. The exception is the Royal Commission on Bilingualism and Biculturalism (1964–65) which recommended that the country be led towards becoming bilingual and bicultural. The federal government took up only the bilingual recommendation in an attempt to forge national unity. Nevertheless, in the form of the Official Languages Act 1969, bilingualism had a huge impact on national English-French relations. By making all federal services bilingual the federal government conceded that francophones were 'partners' in federalism. In separating the language from the culture, however, the Official Languages Act 1969 negated the notion of Quebec as a 'distinct society'. As so often, what seemed to be a gain was to the long-term disadvantage of francophones in Quebec.

In a brief to the Senate in 1978 Professor Dion of Laval University summed up the response. Speaking about the 'Report of the Royal Commission on Bilingualism and Biculturalism' and the 'Pepin-Robarts (Task Force) Report', he said,

> It is a carbon copy. One would think that the same fools had attended the same meeting twice. But what it means is that the same fools are still there . . . Language does not exist by itself, simply because individuals speak it. It needs a social dimension to last and be promising. It seems to me, that any form of language programme . . . must square with the trends of society.[15]

The intense frustration felt by the majority of Québécois at being unable to express their identity was articulated in 1976 by the election of a *Parti Québécois* government in Quebec. In 1980 a province-wide referendum on the issue of sovereignty-association was announced by the provincial government, showing that it believed that the population was ready to assert this claim, and that the federal government would no longer be able to ignore Quebec's demands.

The defeat of the sovereignty-association proposal in the 1980 referendum should not automatically be interpreted as indicative of Québécois satisfaction with the constitutional status quo. Although sovereignty-association was rejected by 60 per cent to 40 per cent, a cultural breakdown of the results revealed that over 50 per cent of francophones had actually voted 'yes'. In short, the meaning of the 'no' vote was ambiguous. The campaign strategy of the 'no' advocates – headed up by the Liberal leader of Quebec, Claude Ryan, and Prime Minister Pierre Trudeau – acknowledged that something was wrong with Quebec's place in the Constitution. The option of simply retaining the status quo was out of the question. In a speech in Montreal Trudeau stated,

I make a solemn declaration to all Canadians in the other provinces: we, the Quebec MPs, are laying ourselves on the line, because we are telling Quebecers to vote 'no' and telling you in the other provinces that we will not agree to your interpreting a 'no' vote as an indication that everything is fine and can remain as it was before.[16]

The referendum, therefore, did not ask Quebec to choose between sovereignty-association and the constitutional status quo, but between sovereignty-association and 'renewed federalism'. Hence, by voting 'no' to sovereignty-association Quebec had voted 'yes' to renewed federalism.[17] Trudeau did not give his 'renewed federalism' a specific definition. In Quebec at least it was, however, a concept with clear implications. As Behiels reasons,

In the last analysis, without undergoing a complete transformation, the system can only go so far as to establish politics aimed at French speaking individuals, not the Québécois nation: bilingualism at the federal level, subsidies to improve employment in certain regions. It is hoped that such measures will resolve a political problem situated at the level of a whole society.[18]

In Trudeau's promise of renewed federalism the Québécois found hope that the 'difference' of Quebec would be constitutionally recognised. As we have seen, this was not a new idea: both the 1840 and 1867 Acts of Parliament had given Quebec some sort of 'distinct society' recognition. The post-World War II period had seen, however, the non-Québécois view of federalism gain dominance over the French-Canadian one, and the Cold War had brought pressures towards centralisation and equalisation. Increased immigration from non-European countries brought a multicultural emphasis rather than a bicultural one. Moreover, Quebec's economic mobilisation demonstrated that the provisions of these Acts no longer protected the 'distinct society' in the late twentieth century. Multiculturalism and economic change had now become processes eroding Québécois identity. Quebec was in danger of becoming a 'French-speaking zone' rather than a 'distinct society'.

For the means to recover the protection and the promotion of the 'distinct society' many in Quebec expected, at the very least, more autonomy in matters of immigration, welfare and economic policy. They also expected an exclusive veto on amendments involving change to the fundamental characteristics of Canada. These expectations were based on the premise, alluded to above by Professor Dion, that 'society' had implications for a wide range of societal life, political, economic and social. It could not be contained within the closed categories of language policy, civil code and education. This premise gave rise to the call for a preamble to the Constitution ensuring that Quebec's 'distinct society' be recognised in the interpretation of that document.

The Constitution is the highest law of Canada and might be supposed, therefore, to capture the essential characteristics of that country, which are embodied in its aspirations, divisions of governmental responsibilities, means of representation and political institutions. If a dispute arises between competing interests, whether they be social, political or economic, the fundamental characteristics are entrenched in the Constitution and can be used, via judicial interpretation, to mediate disputes with impartiality. This method of government, however, is only legitimate as long as the Constitution remains an accurate reflection of the country's characteristics. If certain characteristics – in this case those of Quebec – undergo change, then either the Constitution or the way it is interpreted must also change.

> Rapid change in the status, self-definition and aspirations of important groups may also lead to demands for constitutional change of this [demarcation] sort, to calls for a new social contract or a new set of fundamental premises which will reflect current perceptions of the political community.[19]

In 1982, however, there could be no demarcation of governmental responsibilities or 'powers' because there was increasing evidence that this would not be accepted by anglophone interests. In the mid-1980s the undercurrent of discontent in the under-represented West and among aboriginal peoples was becoming a torrent. Also, if Quebec was recognised as a 'distinct society' the recognition would draw criticism from groups which were tolerant of, if not happy with, the constitutional status quo; for example, francophones living outside Quebec.

The second way of resolving constitutional conflict, according to Simeon and Banting, is by judicial review, where the Constitution's text remains unaltered, but where the courts present a new interpretation of a particular clause or clauses.[20] In 1982, however, this method was fraught with difficulty. The Supreme Court of Canada had an unusually narrow range of judicial powers, being unable to rule unconstitutionality in cases between private citizens and the state. There was a further complication in that one of Quebec's demands pertained to a change in the Supreme Court itself: it wanted *de jure* recognition of the right to have three francophones in the court of nine judges.

Trudeau's proposed solution was to enhance the role of the Supreme

Court by the introduction of the 'Charter of Rights and Freedoms', a constitutionally entrenched document protecting a mixture of individual and collective rights. Within it was Section 33, a clause allowing legislatures to override certain provisions of the Charter, namely Section 2 dealing with fundamental freedoms and Sections 7–15 dealing with legal rights. So, it would draw the courts into the constitutional debate, thus elevating the status of the Supreme Court and judicial review as the means of solving potential constitutional conflict.

The Charter had a second objective:

> to create a national will, a sense of national identity which would lead Canadians to believe that Canada was more than the sum of the wills of the provinces, but had a will of its own.[21]

Despite the popularity of this concept in the anglophone part of the country, it proved to be a dangerous notion to assert during a period of patriation. The fact that Canada would soon, by virtue of an indigenous amending formula, be a wholly sovereign state, no longer obliged to return to Great Britain in order to amend its Constitution, provoked an atmosphere of introspection.[22] Canadians began a critical examination of themselves and their society, seeking to find a rationale for the way they governed themselves, and to discover whether such a 'national will' could exist.

In such an atmosphere the language of rights mobilised the citizenry, and brought into the political culture the notion that the Constitution 'belonged' to the people, rather than governments. The Charter granted people rights that could be abrogated neither by federal nor provincial governments; it spoke to 'the people of Canada' rather than the people of a particular province. This, says Cairns, encouraged the people to think of themselves as 'constitutional actors', without having to use their federal and provincial politicians as 'voices' in constitutional debate.

It should be noted, however, that this development has not diminished Quebec nationalism because this nationalism is now being driven by the business sector; it is no longer sustained solely by the state as it was immediately following the Quiet Revolution.[23] Moreover Quebec has been active in using Section 1 of the Charter, the clause which allows it only to be applied within 'reasonable limits' of democracy, and Section 33, the opt-out clause. This has allowed Quebec a significant degree of Parliamentary control over the application of the Charter.

Despite the federal government's intention that the Charter of Rights and Freedoms should stimulate an individualist liberal ideology at the

expense of Quebec's ambitions,[24] the consequences of rights entrenchment
have been significantly different. In short, tension has emerged between individual and collective rights. The language of rights has been
taken up as much by groups as by individuals, and Sections 25 and 27
(referring to aboriginal and gender rights) more widely used than the
sections dealing with democratic and mobility rights.

The political culture of Canada has tended to emphasise community
over individuality: 'The 1867 Act, devoid of entrenched rights, and
with a clear emphasis on social order, is easily characterised as a
communitarian manifesto of a Burkean kind'.[25] This has meant that
the Charter of Rights and Freedoms has in fact granted certain
collectivities a greater voice by giving them a constitutional meeting
point: rights. This is despite criticism by Quebec politicians that a
Charter would have the opposite effect.[26] Although the Charter tended
to give a role to those groups which were not territorially concentrated, it also gave certain groups the right to educate their children in
either of the official languages *where numbers warranted* (Section 23).
The irony was that the recognition of group rights in the Charter was
an indirect step towards the recognition of a 'distinct society' of Quebec, even though the introduction of a Charter had been intended to
undermine this very possibility.

Constitutional change is more difficult when not only the question
of what changes, but how changes are made, is being discussed . . .
this brings the basis of the federal system under attack.[27]

Having enhanced the role of the courts and the people, there still
remained the original problem: that of formulating an amendment formula for future constitutional change. Apart from a few concessions
to provincial leverage and a very limited acknowledgement that Quebec
was historically 'a province not like the other provinces', there was
no demarcation of power, certainly no 'renewed federalism'. The significance of the Constitution itself, therefore, lay in its 'amending formula'.

In 1981 Trudeau's desire to bring greater democracy to the amending process by means of a referendum was brought down by provincial governments. This may be evidence that challenging elites are
likely to argue for the uniqueness of constitutional questions and call
for a greater role for special institutions.[28]

Trudeau's proposal for the amending formula acknowledged the regional nature of the federation, requiring ratification of an amendment
in six out of ten provinces, including Quebec, Ontario and at least one
Western province and one Maritime province. This too was demol-

ished by the provincial governments. The general formula eventually entrenched allowed for an amendment to be made by

> resolutions of the Senate and House of Commons, and resolutions of the legislative assemblies of at least two-thirds of the provinces that have . . . at least 50% of the population of all the provinces (Section 38).

In refusing Quebec an exclusive veto, the amending formula amounted to a negation of the status of a 'distinct society', and Quebec, of course, refused to sign the Constitution. The amendment had other, more complicated, implications for general participation in the democratic process. These only became apparent five years later when the federal government (through a series of meetings at Meech Lake) attempted to make Quebec a signatory to that Constitution.

The Meech Lake Accord drawn up by Prime Minister Brian Mulroney and the ten provincial Premiers in April 1987 and submitted to the provincial legislatures for ratification, eventually passed its April 1990 deadline still unratified by Manitoba and Newfoundland, and became extinct. Meech Lake's lasting significance was in drawing out patterns in the Canadian polity which Quebec must address if a successful constitutional settlement is to be made.

Its significance was two-fold. First, it reinforced the dynamic relationship between minorities and majorities throughout Canada, and stressed the key role which minorities have in maintaining balance within the federal system. Second, the Accord gave practical expression to a development rooted in the Charter: the lack of a relationship between the decision-makers and the citizenry, a situation which cannot remain if the citizenry continue to demand a role in constitutional politics.

Understanding these relationships is crucial for a successful constitutional settlement in Canada, and neither relationship is independent of the other. The minority groups such as aboriginals, and other excluded groups such as women, will only be successfully accommodated within the Constitution when they can have a voice in the decision-making process. The importance of the minority and majority relationship has been in debate since the British North America Act 1867, when a vital objective of this Act was the suppression of the francophones in Lower Canada. The importance of the second relationship, the citizen and decision-maker relationship has been a more muted development, brought into focus by Quebec's Quiet Revolution, the residual consequence of which was the 1980 referendum.

Understanding the lack of a relationship between the decision-makers and the citizens can be achieved by examining the process surrounding the Meech Lake Accord in the light of the Charter. As has been shown, after April 1982 the Constitution was not only the concern of provinces and Parliament, but also of individuals and groups such as women, ethnic minorities and aboriginal peoples. Through the Charter of Rights and Freedoms these groups had constitutionally entrenched rights. The indirect consequence of this was that legislatures, much less governments, were no longer the sole propagators of constitutional change; the people were too. But the Constitution's amendment clause had condensed democracy rather than expanded it.

As a result, the 1982 Act had made scant framework for citizens to use their new status. With this ambiguity inherent in the Constitution the process of negotiating a new settlement was bound to be difficult and frustrating.

The initial pressure for a Constitutional settlement in 1987 came from the federal government. The federal Conservatives, having won the 1984 election under the leadership of Brian Mulroney, were anxious to bring Quebec back into the constitutional fold, and make sure of Quebec's support over the passage of the contentious 'Free Trade Agreement' (FTA) with the USA. Moreover, Quebec was now governed by a Liberal, Robert Bourassa, who was committed to pursuing Quebec's autonomy within federalism if at all possible. Thus, pressures for the 'distinct society' were strong. The federal government's hopeful objective was that a settlement with Quebec would have no bearing on the interpretation of the Charter, and so it saw no reason to involve the citizens in the process.[29] Anxious to give expression to the Conservative vision of the country as a 'community of communities', however, Mulroney had to invite the provincial governments. These governments seized gladly upon the idea for reasons of their own; they were anxious to regain the power they had lost in the Constitution Act 1982. There were, therefore, strong conflicting objectives even in this elite group.

Since the opening up of the Constitution to the people in 1982, however, and the 'empowering' of groups and individual citizens, a top-down political impetus on its own is unlikely to be sufficient for successful constitutional change. It must be accompanied by a general mobilisation of support at 'grassroots' level to sustain its legitimacy. This was not present in 1987.

Although the Québécois were supportive, having just elected a government with a mandate to negotiate a renewed federalism, other people were not ready for constitutional change. Indeed, the widespread use of the Charter of Rights and Freedoms indicated that, on the contrary, citizens in provinces other than Quebec were pleased with the situation.

The federal government's subsequent decision to proceed alone was influenced by a history of elite-dominated constitutional change which was to prove no longer relevant to the contemporary period. There was a precedent in the 1865 Charlottetown Conference, which also seemed appropriate in 1987. The governments could not wholly be blamed for this; they were merely claiming their inheritance from the ambivalent Constitution Act 1982 whose amendment formula implied that changing the Constitution was the prerogative of government. Coupling this notion with the implications for a weakened Parliamentary role also present in the Constitution Act 1982, the federal government called together the 11 First Ministers to negotiate a new constitutional settlement.

This meeting brought out the tension between elite constitution-making and participatory constitution-making. It ignored the recommendations of the 1987 'MacDonald Report' – a Royal Commission with a mandate to report on Canada's economic future – which contained a volume stressing the need to enhance democracy, thereby involving people in the political process, ultimately reducing large governmental bureaucracies, and making Canada economically competitive.[30] In fact, the process chosen by politicians at Meech Lake also ignored a warning, given in a supplementary paper to the 'Report of the Royal Commission on Bilingualism and Biculturalism' (1967), that elite constitution-making 'transfers to executive bargaining and negotiation what properly belongs to the realm of the [public] political [debate]'.[31]

The move towards notions of participatory democracy, however, made this impossible; indeed, none of the anglophone provincial governments had been elected with a mandate to negotiate constitutional change. The increasing secrecy on the part of the delegates – an indication of fear of public opposition – implied a recognition that ignoring the public had been a mistake.

The criticism of the elite-dominated process revealed the breakdown in the relationship between the provincial governments and the provincial citizens. The accusation that the Meech Lake Accord represented a 'provincialist' view of Canada was made repeatedly.

Aware that their rights had been entrenched in the Constitution in 1982 with some initial reluctance from the provincial governments,[32] women's groups, aboriginals and ethnic minority groups were highly suspicious of a meeting where ten out of eleven Ministers represented provinces, and so their language of protest became confrontational. Moreover, '[the actions of] unsympathetic politicians are still too fresh in the memories of national women's organisations for them not to be suspicious of a deal struck in private by eleven men', stated a delegate to the Special Joint Committee.[33] The sense of non-involvement was reiterated: 'This committee is hearing from many different groups which say: "But we are not involved; we are left out and we feel the accord is something that has been created at our expense"'.[34]

Not only did these groups, which in many cases have pan-Canadian constituencies rather than being localised and provincial, find themselves unable to trust their premiers, but they also felt betrayed by the federal system. They perceived that Mulroney, for the sake of political expediency, was acting as the representative of Quebec rather than in the national interest. Although this alienated them even further from the debate, it gave them the role of protectors of the 'national interest', a strong rallying point to which other Canadians could flock. It also gave them the figure-head of Pierre Trudeau, still massively influential, who said that the Accord negated 'a sense of national belonging . . . a sense of one nation'.[35]

Depriving these groups of any part in the process or even a spokesperson in the negotiations meant that the citizens' contribution to the debate over the ratification became increasingly parochial. In the absence of a national viewpoint everyone, it seemed, felt driven to speak out on behalf of his or her own interest group, and not for the nation as a whole. The pressure was on for as many interest groups as possible to voice their discontent, making it more and more difficult to identify where the real issues lay.

That the Meech Lake Accord was finally brought down by Elijah Harper, a Cree Indian and a member of the Manitoban legislature, was symbolic.[36] Against all the odds, it seemed that one representative of countless people shut out by the elite-dominated process managed to break through in the Manitoban legislature and make aboriginal opinions heard. It was a pivotal event, showing that Meech Lake had failed because its formulators failed to accommodate those people to whom the Constitution now 'belonged'. For them the debate was about federalist concerns, primarily divisions of power, and no doubt their will would have triumphed through the elite process had not the two visions of the Constitution overlapped. Canadian federalism is inextricably tied up with the issue of minority concerns and, indeed, the Meech Lake Accord's *raison d'être* was the struggle of Canada's most important minority with federalism. It was almost inevitable, therefore, that those minorities with new-found status, but with no debating place in the federal system, would struggle even harder to achieve such a place.

The Accord also failed because the national relationship between minorities and majorities was no longer simply that of a francophone minority to an anglophone majority. This increasingly complex relationship was emphasised in the Meech Lake process. By assenting to Quebec's 'distinct society' demands, the Accord conceded the point that the Québécois, as a national minority within a provincial boundary, were inadequately protected and promoted. This is linked to questions about how, and why, minorities should be protected. Secondly, the fact that this minority happened to constitute an overwhelming majority at a provincial level raised another set of questions about the nature of provincial equality and the place of provinces within the federal system. Thus, Quebec posed a challenge to the fundamental characteristics of the federal system.

It may be claimed that federal systems are usually put in place to enable efficient government to be upheld in a country with great population and cultural diversity. This may be on the basis of geography, ethnicity, culture and all other criteria which cause one group of people to be different from another. A federal system recognises that each homogenous group may not necessarily have the same interests or the same way of governing its people. It can accommodate this by erecting territorial barriers around a group and giving it relative autonomy through certain powers of jurisdiction; the group which is a national minority is protected because it has became a provincial majority. In the Canadian model, provincial equality has been, apart from a few significant exceptions (which have already been mentioned), maintained on the basis of allocating the same powers to each province, believing that the way they use them will develop each provincial character. According 'distinct society' status to Quebec in Meech Lake represented the culmination of a challenge to that basis, such that the 'equal provinces, equal powers' notion was negated completely.

Addressing this challenge to notions of provincial equality was only part of the work to be done before Quebec's successful recognition as a 'distinct society'; another part concerned the provincial minorities. Provincial minorities are inevitable in a federal system which defines its 'provinces' on a territorial basis, since migration patterns in the industrialised world ensure that contemporary societies are rarely homogenous. The two-tier federal system tends not to protect their interests, and minority groups might feel subject to domination by the majority in their provinces unless they had a higher political authority than that of the province to protect them.

In some countries, including the USA, the structure of the federal system offers little protection to these minorities; trying to do so would be an impossible task, a never-ending 'Russian Doll' where the recognition of one minority merely reveals the existence of another, smaller, one. In Canada, however, the commitment in Confederation to give French educational provision to francophone minorities had, over the years, given the federal government a role in the protection of minority interests. The natural progression of this principle in 'multicultural' late twentieth-century Canada meant that the federal government had an inherent responsibility for the protection of minority interests in general.

Hence other minorities, as well as the Québécois, came to expect Charter protection. When, in 1982, the Charter extended protection for the linguistic minorities of the founding partners, and gave it also to minorities and groups which were not territorially defined, by implication the federal government became their constitutional protector too. Yet this responsibility was not upheld in the 1987 process: instead, the federal government assumed a role as a protector of a provincial majority, the Québécois, disrupting the precarious balance between majorities and minorities and provoking widespread criticism of the Accord.

'Let us first take a look at history ... Quebec has always been a distinct society ... and that is why Quebec has to be recognised by the Constitution as a distinct society'.[37] If, as Louis Balthazer says, the Meech Lake Accord, by giving the Québécois 'nation' constitutional recognition as a 'distinct society', was restoring its historical legitimacy, then aboriginals, francophones outside Quebec and anglophones within Quebec, should also be given this historical recognition, argued their spokespeople. While aboriginals saw the 'distinct society' clause as 'trying to "freeze out" the participation of the north',[38] non-Québécois francophones feared it was a move toward unilingualism which would weaken the incentive of other provinces to protect their francophone minorities. Similarly, the anglophone minority in Quebec believed the 'distinct society' clause would be detrimental to their status and, therefore, its main party, 'Alliance Quebec', attached allegiance to the former national objective of bilingualism.

The objections of these minority groups demonstrated that the constitutional change had another, social, dimension. Whereas the federal government in 1987 saw the Constitution as an instrument to gain their political objectives, and whereas the provinces saw it as a document which secured and clarified their power, the electorate saw the Constitution 'as an instrument of community formation and social management'.[39] The various groups used the document to try to meet their own objectives. Having constitutional protection and rights gives a group status in the polity, and any threat to that status naturally aroused an indignant reaction. George Erasmus of Alliance Quebec told the Senate,

> You cannot deal with the rights of some Canadians without affecting the rights of others. If you upgrade the rights of the French and do not do the same to the rights of everyone else, by definition, you have just lowered everyone else's.[40]

One may conclude that the 'Meech Lake' process demonstrated how difficult constitutional agreement would be now that many different groups were looking for representation in the Constitution. 'Meech Lake' brought the state of Canadian society into focus for the population of Canada and those who governed it. The failure of the Accord showed that it was no longer possible to address one group's 'problems' exclusively. This is contrary to Leslie, whose defence of 'Meech Lake' argues that 'for moral reasons' Quebec's constitutional agenda must be tackled before anything else.[41] Thus, the Meech Lake process reaffirmed the federal government's responsibility for all minorities, and that it must, therefore, listen to them. But it also told them that it must go beyond listening to them, and allow them to participate in future constitutional change. The Constitution would then be seen, not as a document of social management which separates groups and has divisive effects, a 'family portrait' as it were,[42] but rather, a document of integration, a means by which constitutional priorities could be assessed and a sense of the needs of the Canadian nation could emerge.

The Charlottetown Agreement 1992, like the Meech Lake Accord, represented a consensus reached between the Prime Minister and the provincial Premiers, this time with the addition of business and aboriginal leaders.

The fundamental difference between 'Charlottetown' and 'Meech Lake' was that the Charlottetown Agreement was drawn up in a more democratic manner and with much more openness – including the use of televised hearings – than the Meech Lake Accord. In November 1990 the Mulroney federal government had set up a 'Citizen's Forum on Canada's Future' and a working group, the 'Beaudoin-Edwards Committee' to 'provide the basis for a broad public discussion and full opportunity for public participation on Canada's constitutional future'.[43] Quebec had already given a constitutional mandate to the 'Allaire Committee', which visited every constituency in the province, presenting the constitutional options in various media forms.[44]

The Quebec National Assembly set up its own working group, the 'Bélanger-Campeau Commission' and also agreed to hold a referendum on the constitutional future of Quebec by the end of October 1992. Mulroney did not announce a national referendum on the consensus until much later. This shows that Quebec was still ahead of anglophone Canada in learning 'Meech Lake's lessons about expanded democracy. Nevertheless, Quebec failed, as Russell points out, to include aboriginal representatives in the Commission's membership of 36.[45] Instead of full participatory democracy in the process of constitutional change, there was only selective participatory democracy which may have made this process less valid.

The results of these constitutional commissions showed clearly that an agreement similar to the 1992 Charlottetown Accord would be welcomed neither in Quebec nor in the rest of Canada. Jean Allaire's Committee reported that the Québécois wanted greater political autonomy with economic links, and the Bélanger-Campeau Commission, while non-committal, did at least identify that 'profound changes must be made to Quebec's political and constitutional status' and still maintained that the arrangements articulated in Meech Lake were 'minimal conditions' for signing the Constitution.[46] By contrast, the federal government's Citizen's Forum found that English-Canada drew the line at any further decentralisation of power, and in fact wanted 'a strong government ... to remedy economic ills ...'.[47] The reports were reaffirming what the popular press had been publishing since 1990. Merely two months before the Accord was drawn up, *Macleans* magazine had emphatically stated, 'there remains significant public opposition throughout the West to the idea of giving Quebec special powers'.[48] So, even before negotiations began, it was evident that the aspirations of Quebec and the rest of the country were not at all congruent. The fact that the government ignored the reports' findings suggests that, although the citizenry was being allowed to participate through the voicing of its views, subsequently these views were not regarded.

Since the negotiators at Charlottetown sensed they were not in line with the mood of the general population, they did not have the confidence to listen to other approaches to the Constitution. Six months previously, former Ontario Premier David Peterson had suggested that the traditional 'difficulties' of Canada must be seen as positive differences before an agreement could be reached. 'Consensus', he said, was not about 'learning to live with our inherited problems', but about 'enough spontaneous acts of generosity and kindness ... to save the country'.[49]

Generosity was not, it might be said, a characteristic of the Charlottetown Accord. The Western provinces did not receive the 'Triple E' Senate they had demanded. Although the Senate was to be *elected* and *equal* – each province to elect six Senators – it was not to be *effective:* the Charlottetown Consensus stated, 'The Senate should not be a confidence chamber'.[50] Quebec, too, was discontented: although it received a guarantee of at least 25 per cent of House of Commons seats, the 'Canada Clause' failed to affirm the role of the federal government to 'preserve and protect the distinct society of Quebec'. It was 'a very very much reduced "distinct society" compared to Meech', according to *Parti Québécois* leader Jacques Parizeau, whose criticism of the Quebec Premier was both imaginative and bitter: 'I was far from thinking that Robert Bourassa would come back so happy . . . he is asking, "How do you want to be eaten; skewered, grilled, boiled, or with 'sauce béchamel'?"'.

Although the federal and provincial governments campaigned fiercely on its behalf, the inadequacy of the Accord came across in the guarded tones of the Prime Minister and the provincial Premiers.[51] 'Manitoba will support changes to the amending formula only if the Senate package is approved', warned Premier Gary Filmon.[52] Mulroney, equally defensive, clearly anticipated charges of betrayal from minority groups:

Proposals for guaranteed representation (for Quebec) came from Western provinces and others. Provinces will be able to choose election method of senators; circumstances may see provinces choose senators differently; however they will have to respect federal law.[53]

Given that it was introduced in this negative framework, the rejection of the Accord in the October 1992 referendum was not surprising.

In a federal system a consensus between interest groups can seldom be reached if they are unequally matched, and Quebec and English-speaking Canada fall into this category. Although Bourassa signed the Charlottetown Consensus in the name of Quebec, a look at the state of Quebec society and its governmental policies in 1992 tells us that in spirit Quebec never signed the Consensus. A significant proportion of the Quebec Liberal Party were dismayed at Bourassa's perceived betrayal of Quebec by his quiet alliance with Mulroney, and acceptance of the weakened 'Canada Clause' in the Charlottetown round. In 1994 the new 'sovereigntist' party, the *Parti de l'Action démocratique* (PADQ) was formed, being derived principally from the Quebec Liberal Party's youth wing.[54] Little over six months after its founding convention, the *Parti de l'Action démocratique* had sufficient support and mobilisation to win a seat in the September 1994 provincial election.

The optimism and confidence of the *Parti de l'Action démocratique* symbolises the current direction of Quebec nationalism. This new party has risen quickly, probably because it appeals to a strong Quebec nationalism which is rooted in political and economic pragmatism. By contrast, the separatist *Parti Québécois* government, although it confidently presented a draft bill on Quebec's sovereign status and held a referendum on the final version of this bill in October 1995, did not have the mandate it seems to have anticipated. In the September 1994 election, while the *Parti Québécois* took more than 61 per cent of the 125 seats in the National Assembly, it did not obtain a majority of the popular vote: 44.7 per cent of the electorate voted for the *Parti Québécois*, closely followed by the 44.3 per cent which voted for the Quebec Liberals.[55]

Moreover, the *Parti Québécois*, which came to power on a reformist social-democratic platform, was in a paradoxical situation. Its draft bill was deemed by many to be a 'joy-ride', assuming continued use of Canadian currency and passports, and continued adherence to Canada's foreign treaties, including NAFTA.[56] The *Parti Québécois* did not acknowledge the need to gain the federal government's acquiescence on these matters (a potentially futile task, given the depth of anti-Quebec feeling in parts of the West). Neither did the Quebec government present sufficient evidence that it had accommodated aboriginal demands for self-government into its plans. This has been an issue of unprecedented importance since the inclusion of self-government demands in the Charlottetown Consensus. Moreover, stalling over the timing of the referendum confirmed that Parizeau had become aware of these inadequacies in the draft bill. The paradox was that, although Parizeau's mandate to negotiate such change was questionable, he had taken his draft bill to the people, through 15 regional commissions set up throughout Quebec – cleverly said the cynics – as a way of reducing the influence of the federalist stronghold, Montreal island. Since most of the commissioners were avowed sovereigntists, it was debatable whether they would all make an entirely unbiased record of what they had heard. Even so, they were not able to present the government with a clear-cut answer on sovereignty: there were too many other issues which could be brought into the debate, not least the aboriginal question.

Although this was the case, the Quebec government had firmly pledged to go ahead with the October 1995 referendum. Indeed, a 'Yes' vote was not unthinkable, given that only a simple majority was required, that more than 50 per cent of francophones had voted 'Yes' in 1980, and that French language education had become (and remains) much stronger since that time.

A 'Yes' vote, however, would not have signalled the start of an easy run to sovereignty, although the *Parti Québécois* government would have probably interpreted it in this way. Rather, a 'Yes' to sovereignty would have merely affirmed a gradual process of economic and cultural separation which has been nurtured by Quebec nationalism since the Quiet Revolution. It would not necessarily have been an indication that political separation was imminent or would easily be achieved. The contemporary nationalism of Quebec is, however, being driven by all sectors of society, and is potentially stronger than the nationalism of the 1960s. The Quebec Liberal Party's 1985 report 'Mastering Our Future' identified with the Quiet Revolution's heritage by saying that, 'There is a close link between the entrepreneurial urge . . . and the feelings of confidence that spring from belonging to a respected society and from active participation in a dynamic culture'.[58] It described Quebec's 'most urgent challenge' as 'under employment of our human resources', and a 'competitive economy' as the first of four 'master trump cards'. The success of this challenge can be seen in the fact that the majority of members of the 1992 Bélanger-Campeau Commission were business-people, whereas in former times they would have been politicians.

In the post-Meech Lake era this expansionary attitude is developing still further. In the 1960s Quebec focused on education, particularly the setting up of French-speaking universities, in a recognition that education was the key to economic development. In the contemporary period Quebec is seeking to boost its economic evolution by encouraging specific vocational training. The Quebec government's 1991 'Policy Statement on Labour Force Development' concluded that, 'Our rapidly changing economy and the increasingly important role of the labour force require . . . commitment to the highest standards of skills development'.[59] The report emphasised that this was not a final goal, but merely a 'point of departure' which would, therefore, give nationalism a strong industrial base.

The main body of the report demonstrated how this socio-economic base could be transposed into a nationalist base. There was the policy of repatriation: first, of funds allocated by the federal government to the labour sector; second, of 'all labour force development programmes and services that we do not already own'; and third, of 'responsibilities [that] will only be repatriated following negotiations concerning the transfer of federal employees to the *Société québécoise de developpement de la main-d'oeuvre*'.[60] A consequence of these policies, a stronger version of which has been put in place by the *Parti Québécois* government, might be a simultaneous loss of influence in Ottawa and withdrawal into Quebec for the Québécois. It could only have detrimental effects for bilingualism and the 'distinct society' of francophone minorities. Since its aspirations are not inter-provincial, but international, Quebec is, apparently, unconcerned by this. While the rest of the country is predominantly concerned with its internal problems, Quebec is withdrawing from debate over these matters, including issues concerning other francophone minorities. It has a wider vision and is cultivating links with the francophone world. In the 1960s links were merely cultural, almost symbolic; in the contemporary period, however, when a significant proportion of Québécois do not have French cultural origins, the links are strongly economic.[61] Indeed, the 'Mastering Our Future' report named these links as its second 'trump card', and in 1991 the Quebec government had this to say on the subject:

> The world over, barriers to economic exchange are toppling one by one. Freer world trade has also led to the development of more, and more complete, free-trade zones in Europe and North America. Any society seeking growth must belong to an economy which extends beyond national boundaries and participates fully in the globalization of markets. The sweeping liberalisation of trade has encouraged states to associate more closely in order to open their borders to trade and jointly seek development and economic prosperity.[62]

Since the Quiet Revolution the Québécois have had high expectations of their society. It seems that they are likely to fulfil their economic expectations, and not for the sake of francophone minorities elsewhere, and certainly not for its anglophone minority, will they restrict the development of Quebec.

In 1979 the 'Task Force on Canadian Unity' made the statement: 'We believe that Canadians have a long way to travel, and little time to make the journey'.[63] In the ensuing years, up until the present day, Canadians have travelled a long way and the path they have taken is one of increased participation in constitutional affairs. They clearly have not reached the end of that journey: Quebec and the rest of Canada, along with the Québécois and anglophone people, remain in constitutional discord. Quebec continues to be a non-signatory to the Constitution Act 1982. Whether or not the time required to bring Quebec into the Constitution has run out remains ambiguous. If it has, on the one hand, then a constitutional stalemate has been reached, and Quebec may have no option but to separate from Canada if it desires to continue the development it has experienced in recent years. On the other hand, if time has not run out, then there may still be a place within the Canadian Confederation for a Quebec which is a 'distinct society'.

Along the 'journey' the governments of both Quebec and the rest of Canada have empowered their people with a greater voice in constitutional matters: first Quebec, by calling a referendum on sovereignty-association in 1980, and then the federal government, by empowering all Canadians with rights in the Charter of Rights and Freedoms in April 1982. Having gained a voice with which to articulate ideas, the expectation of participation soon followed as a matter of course. By 1987, when the federal government under Prime Minister Mulroney came to helping the Québécois attain constitutional status as a 'distinct society', other groups were sufficiently mobilised to inject their own aspirations onto the agenda.

Consequently, the Meech Lake Accord reached its deadline still unratified, hindering the realisation of Quebec's aspirations and encouraging it to withdraw from mainstream affairs in the federal system. By 1992 the federal government had realised that it was necessary to draw minority groups into the constitutional process. Unfortunately, however, the text of the Charlottetown Consensus did not reflect the views expressed in consultation. The result was a deepening of the cynicism with which both the Western provinces and Quebec viewed the federal government, a cynicism which expressed itself in the unequivocal removal of the Progressive Conservatives in the October 1993 general election.[64] The new Liberal government initially downplayed the constitutional impasse, Prime Minister Chrétien declaring that he would leave 'constitutional issues on the backburner'.[65] Indeed, Quebec is still ahead of the federal government in incorporating its people into the constitutional process, although it is closely followed by the West.[66]

The expansion of democracy in Canada, through increased participation and provincial hearings, has revealed that Canadians are 'travelling two different roads'.[67] This problem has grown more evident since the rejection of the Charlottetown Consensus, and will have to be addressed before an acceptable constitutional settlement can be found. While the Québécois, as an increasingly politically active people, have been travelling towards greater autonomy since the 1960s, the people of 'the rest of Canada' (TROC), predominantly anglophone, have begun to articulate their own objectives more strongly in the last 15 years. As this chapter has aimed to show, these are not homogenous

objectives: aboriginals demand self-government, and there are also separatist pressures in British Columbia, while the West generally is 'holding
out' for greater representation in the Senate in the context of an over-
haul of the Parliamentary system. Central Canadians, moreover, contend that their interests are best served by a strong central government.
All these groups have been politically mobilised and motivated by a
Charter of Rights and Freedoms, expressing both group and individual
rights. For predominantly anglophone Canada, therefore, the Charter
deprioritised the cause for a constitutionally entrenched 'distinct society' and has made it 'prepared to contemplate a new community
exclusive of Quebec'.[68] The gap between the two roads, therefore, grows
wider as the two nationalisms develop.

CONCLUSION

If Quebec is becoming increasingly distant from the Canadian state,
with growing autonomy, then what are the implications of this? Native Canadian separatism has been officially sanctioned, with notional
autonomy granted to native peoples, while the West is increasingly
vociferous for further decentralisation.

Combined, these separatist movements within Canada may well have
the effect of fundamentally changing the character of the Canadian
state. At the very least, a confederation of autonomous regions may
replace the unitary state. If such a change occurs – and it would seem
to be underway already – then, as we saw in Chapter 2, there is a
strong possibility of it having political repercussions in the USA. Cultural differences and divergent political histories might be supposed
by some to make such an effect unlikely, but this may be illusory as
we saw in the previous chapter also. Cultural differences separating
Americans from Canadians, rather than between cultures and regions
within the two present states, may be declining and trends within the
USA could produce culturally distinct and potentially separatist zones,
some of which might cross the present US–Canadian border.

This and the previous chapter have identified patterns in present events
which might be expected to continue into the near future. The importance of these trends to the questions of US decline and political instability in the Americas depends upon the extent to which they persist
and become more accentuated.

The crucial problem with the use of such trends to evaluate future
developments has always been the same: which trends will persist and

which will fail? In the next chapter a solution to this problem is offered, by proposing that primary and enduring characteristics can be recognised in the political and cultural development of any state through the detailed analysis of its early political and cultural history. This may enable the calibration of trend analysis and the logical projection of selected trends into the future.

In order to examine this hypothesis, data from Latin America will be used to form a test case and then the approach will be applied to the USA. First, however, it will be necessary to set out the basis of this new approach.

4 The Legacy of State-Formation in the Contemporary Politics of the Americas

While it has been possible to identify many trends towards separatism and social collapse in contemporary North America, it is much more difficult to assess which of these trends will prove significant in future. This has long been the most pressing problem of all attempts to use trend analysis in the study of international relations.

History shows that some trends identifiable in one historical period, or even in one decade, continue unchanged into the next, while some fade out, others become less important and yet others are accentuated. If trend analysis is to be a valuable tool in the evaluation of future global prospects there has to be some resolution of this question, if only to a limited degree of reliability.

This is the issue that will be addressed in this chapter, which examines a new approach to the resolution of this problem, in relation to the political development of the Americas. In doing so, it will propose the view that it is possible to identify primary and enduring characteristics, shaped by the very process of state-formation, which are constant aspects of the political culture of each state.

It will be argued on theoretical grounds that, as these characteristics continue to play a role in modern political cultures,[1] they can be used to assess the relative likelihood of the persistence, or discontinuation, of trends identified on the basis of contemporary and recent data. This is a hypothesis which itself is clearly amenable to historical evaluation.

In order to illustrate this approach, prior to its application to the specific case of the USA, it is examined in relation to examples from Latin America. This both serves to elucidate the approach itself and has the additional benefit of helping to explain the basis of regional and national difference among the states in the Americas.

First, however, it is necessary to introduce the theoretical basis of this chapter. Perhaps it is worth noting that this perspective might be of interest to other scholars working on the question of global change, in other regions or in relation to very different issues.

THE ENDURING SIGNIFICANCE OF STATE-FORMATION[2]

Recent years have seen the development of a distinct branch of mathematics and biology given over to the study of complexity. In this context, complexity refers to the differentiation and the degree of structuring of the entity under study. For example, the structure and differentiation between its parts seen in a biological organism, such as a plant, enables us to say that it is a complex organism. Mathematical approaches to complexity have stressed several important properties of the emergence and character of complex systems. These properties can be expressed in both mathematical and conceptual terms, and it is the latter approach which will be employed here. So the use of mathematics as a basis for theory in this case is analogous to the way in which mathematical approaches to systems theory have been incorporated in a conceptual rather than mathematical form into the social sciences.

Of the properties of complex systems, as seen in mathematics, two features are of special note here. First and most importantly, there is the concept of 'initial states'. This proposes that very minor fluctuations in the exact circumstances of origin of a complex system can, over time, produce great divergences in its form. That is, structure and differentiation can be transformed by minor differences in the specifics of their origin. Importantly, a corollary of this is that complex systems retain features deriving from the exact character of their origins as an enduring part of their form.

Second is the theory of 'extreme sensitivity', usually referred to colloquially as the 'butterfly effect'. In this view, subsequent minor fluctuations in any part of the system can produce great changes overall, again exhibiting an amplifying effect over time. Yet, these changes can be over-ridden by a hierarchy of structured responses such as those deriving from the initial state of the system.

These two perspectives, although mathematical in basis, both stress the importance of 'historical' specifics and, most of all, of the specifics of origins in shaping the form of systems. If we see socio-political institutions, such as states, as complex systems, then these approaches are plainly of interest to the political scientist. This is not to say that other dynamical factors are incapable of over-riding such properties of complex systems, but the possibility exists that these types of factors are at work in structuring short-term events in political history if we concede that states are complex systems.

To make such a claim, it must be stressed, is not to see change in human societies and institutions as operating according to mathematical laws on a mechanistic basis. Non-linear dynamics, which lie at the core of the mathematics of complexity, propose that such logic cannot be identified in complex systems, nor do they suggest a return to behaviouralist approaches.

The problem with complex systems which exhibit extreme sensitivity is, of course, that they are liable to be highly unstable and constantly changing. Historical knowledge and everyday experience show us that political institutions are not like this, yet in mathematical terms they would have to be classified as 'complex'. Clearly, there is a constraining factor, or factors, which over-ride this tendency to change, yet which still permit less frequent major changes to occur. An answer to this apparent paradox may be based on the observation that change in all political institutions derives from decision-making, and this takes place in a matrix of beliefs, cultural factors, perceptions and other constraints upon action. As Giddens has pointed out, these 'structures' constrain human decision-making, and also frequently 'enable' it: the relationship between them and decision-making is often both reflexive and contextual. Of these factors, some can remain constants through time and these, given their potential to constrain decision-making and therefore to limit the volatility of complex political institutions, are especially relevant here. Political and cultural structures, often interacting together in historical contexts to produce a 'political culture', within which decisions are made and change can occur, can, therefore, have the effect of shaping the way that a political institution changes through time. by acting as the structural context of decision-making, so as to produce regularities in the sequence of political events. Here may lie the basis of a solution to the paradox of why political institutions are complex (in the mathematical sense) but also frequently show a high degree of stability over time. Yet, the role of political culture (and of culture in general) as a constraint on decision-making itself must be affected by the theory of complexity according to this model: if political institutions are mathematically complex then so too will be many aspects of political culture. These will also be shaped by the exact circumstances of their origin, but constrained by their own internal structures. So, the origin of the political culture of a state under study, and of the state itself, must be studied together in order for us to evaluate the aspects of that situation which may yield recurrent regularities in its subsequent political and cultural history sufficient to shape trends in its future development.

Consequently, in the search for a theory of trend analysis which enables us to calibrate trend projection in a logical way, we may employ both these aspects together, adapting the theory of complexity for our own purposes as political scientists and historians rather than using it simply 'off the peg' as if human societies were biological organisms. In practice, this means that we must seek the 'initial state' of a political institution, the development of which we want to analyse, but examine the early history both of that institution (here a state) and of the cultural matrix within which it originated. In this way we may both solve the apparent paradox of non-volatile, complex, political institutions and enable a calibration of observed trends: if a trend can be shown to be an outcome of cultural regularities integrated with the state since its origins, then the 'initial state' of both of these aspects will enable us to project that trend into the future. There has, of course, to be the proviso that if this culture were to change, the observed regularity may (and probably would) cease to be of relevance.

While these approaches might be of use in many contexts, here they will be employed to examine the role of state-formation in the shaping of subsequent political history. To do so, one may allow consideration not merely of the circumstances of formal state-formation itself, but of the very early (formative) history of the state to be taken into account. Consequently, evidence is used here from the first 50 years of each state's history as indicative of its formative stage: its 'initial state'.

In order to evaluate the validity of this approach prior to its application to the case of the USA, it may be useful to examine evidence from the political history of Latin America. This analysis will, of course, aim to evaluate whether the circumstances of the formative stage of state-formation have played a continuing role in shaping characteristics still fundamental to the political history of the states examined.

STATE-FORMATION AND POLITICAL IDENTITY IN ARGENTINA AND PERU[3]

Both Argentina and Peru give us examples of states which show strong tendencies to comply with the expectations of an 'initial states' hypothesis regarding their political history.

Argentina was originally part of the same Spanish imperial province as Peru, so their divergent subsequent history is an especially interesting test case of this theory. When independence was achieved in the 1820s, this was not an especially destructive episode in the history of Argentina. Instead, it resulted in a strong tradition of militarism as a response to the resounding defeat of the Spanish imperialists and, to a lesser extent, of an Argentinian nationalism. The subsequent state was characterised by a maintenance of the political dominance of the land-owning aristocracy and a trend towards unification and centralisation soon emerged, exemplified during the period of Juan Manuel de Rosan in the nineteenth century.

The elimination of armed irregulars (the so-called *caudillos*) and the terrorisation of political opponents to the regime in control were accompanied by an efficient bureaucratic administration and a developed sense of national identity, spilling over into a tendency to nationalism. The stability produced by the ease of transition to independence and the efficiency of the administrative framework promoted economic growth, and this characterised Argentinian history during the late nineteenth century.

Despite this economic growth, the trends of militarism and nationalism led to Argentina being involved in war with its neighbours and the control of the state by military leaders during the nineteenth century. The ease of the transition to independence also assisted the retention of an essentially 'European' culture, and economic development led to an influx of immigrants and the subsequent growth of a substantially European-born and relatively wealthy lower class in contrast to other Latin-American countries.

These political and cultural characteristics were all established in the initial stage of the state's development and can be seen to have played an important role in its political history. For example, the Peronist regime, with its militarist and nationalist agendas, exemplified many of these aspects, while the so-called 'military phase' of the country's political development, following the coup of 1966, also exhibited these traits.

At present, the restoration of democracy following the disastrous Falklands adventure, has led to the downplaying of the military dimension of this political culture, but the army remains a strong force in Argentinian politics. Likewise, Menem's Argentina still shows strongly nationalistic and Europeanist tendencies, the latter despite the Syrian background of its President.

One may contrast the situation in Argentina with that of Peru. Here, the initial problem of state-formation was not the emergence of nationalism, but the low level of national identity. Unlike Argentina, the population of Peru was principally not culturally European and ethnically only 10 per cent of the population today is European in background. Other characteristics of Peru's early political history as an independent state are clearly identifiable. First, there is the matter of debt and foreign investment. Since the acquisition of a British loan of £1.8 million as early as 1822, the nation's economy has been severely indebted to banks in the Northern hemisphere. By the 1920s, foreign investors held, for example, a virtual monopoly on credit in Peru.

Another characteristic already established during the period of state-formation was the role of the military. The state took its subsequent form during a series of military coups between 1828 and the 1840s. In the 1870s and 1880s, militarism involved the state in the War of the Pacific in which it was disastrously defeated but, despite this, military rule survived until the early 1890s. Even after the following period of civilian oligarchy, another military-backed dictatorship took control from 1919 until the 1920s, and in 1930 another coup imposed military rule.

Although the dictator, Cerro, was subsequently elected in 1931, he was assassinated in 1933 and another general took over control. Civilian rule only became established in 1939, but another coup, in 1948, led to yet another period of military government. While free elections returned in 1956, repression continued into the 1960s, with vicious measures being imposed to curb dissent. A coup followed in 1968, leading to military government in 1975 and, even then, another general – who was also a descendant of an earlier President – took control.

The democratic elections of 1980 led to an elected civilian government, but the infamous debt crisis of the 1980s was fully established by this time. Plainly, in a state indebted to Northern-hemisphere banks for more than 150 years, the traits which characterised state-formation continued to be felt in the present period in the national economy.

A 'CONTROL': MEXICO[4]

It might be argued that these two examples, despite their apparent attestation of the importance of 'initial states' in political history, are inadequate to illustrate the validity of this theory. This is because both states derive from a very similar background. While this might alternatively be interpreted as giving strong support to the validity of the theory of initial states in political analysis, in that it shows the continuing significance of minor variations in the circumstances of state-formation, it is useful to examine a further example before a more detailed application of the theory is attempted. For this 'control' Mexico forms a useful example, as its political background is unconnected with state-formation in Argentina and Peru.

Mexico's independence resulted in disorder and decay, with much of the new state in economic ruin. While the Spaniards were expelled by force, armed bands (*caudillos*) now attempted to seize political control. Culturally and ethnically mixed, the social and ruling elite were ostentatious in their display of wealth and status and a polarised society was established with opulence and poverty co-existing. Political instability between 1821 and 1860 led to more than 50 Presidents in that time, of whom 35 were backed by the military. This, in turn, enabled the *caudillos* to seize control of the state by force and to attempt to ransack the economy, while leaving the government to the civil service and other professional groups.

The resulting period of political instability led both to the independence of Texas (1835–45) and the Mexican–American war (called by Mexicans the 'War of the North American Invasion'). In the early twentieth century, further political instability accompanied by armed insurrection followed, as exemplified by the Mexican Revolution.

Today, similar economic and political problems still characterise Mexico. Social and economic inequalities are aggravated by extreme economic dependence on the USA, with which 60 per cent of Mexican trade takes place, and a major foreign debt burden. Armed insurrection continues, with periods of guerrilla warfare in the 1970s and 1990s.

Thus, in Mexico – as in Argentina and Peru – the circumstances of state-formation and the early political history of the state, still play an important role today. The relative lack of guerrilla warfare in mid-twentieth-century Mexico alerts us to an interesting aspect of this pattern, however: these are recurrent, not continuous, characteristics. Despite this, some such characteristics may be near-continuous aspects of political history. In each of these cases, the theory of 'initial states' would seem, at least as a broad generalisation, to hold true. Interestingly, through this preliminary study we can also see the basis for the emergence and maintenance of diverse regional political cultures in the Americas, and clarify the way in which early political history has shaped the subsequent differential development of the continent.

Having conducted a brief examination of the validity of this approach, it is now possible to turn to a more detailed application directly related to the central theme of this book.

THE CASE OF THE USA

To examine the implications of this theory for questions of political instability and the prospects for future developments in America, one must look in detail at the formation, and early political and cultural history, of the USA. On this basis it will be hoped to establish those fundamental characteristics of US political culture which shape the present development of the USA and are liable to continue to play a significant part in their future.

By incorporating political development with an examination of early American social, economic, demographic and religious history, it may be possible to encompass in this approach an evaluation of the role which those aspects of American life have played in shaping the political history of the American empire. This may be of help in assessing whether current trends deriving from such factors are likely to persist into the twenty-first century.

In order to undertake this analysis it is important to separate preconceptions about early American history and well-evidenced historical 'fact'. The early history of the USA is a subject of much preconceived opinion both in the USA and elsewhere, not all of which is an accurate depiction of historical reality. Most of all, there is a tendency to misperceive the character of the American colonies at the time of the Revolution.

In order to understand the circumstances of American state-formation it is necessary to begin in the colonial period, and to define those characteristics which had already formed prior to the American Revolution. By 1776 the political culture of the USA had already taken shape, so it is in this period of development that the 'initial state' of US state-formation must be sought. Consequently, it will be necessary here to give a history of pre-Revolutionary America and then relate this to the period of state-formation. In this way, the origins of US political culture and the trends shaping it can be more clearly defined and its primary characteristics identified.

STATE-FORMATION AND POLITICAL CULTURE IN THE USA[5]

Although it was the English who founded the American colonies, later to become the USA, they were late to settle in North America. Despite John Cabot's 'discovery' of Newfoundland in 1497, they did not establish themselves in North America until nearly a century later, when the English Crown was in a strong enough economic position to challenge Spanish and Portuguese hegemony in the New World. In 1585 Elizabeth I gave Walter Raleigh support to set up a colony on Roanoke Island. Although he hoped to accost unsuspecting Spanish merchants on their way back to Spain, this proved unsuccessful and, in 1586, the colonists returned to England, demoralised by harsh conditions. The following year a similar attempt to place settlers at Roanoke resulted in their unfortunate disappearance without trace. It was more than 20 years before another attempt was made at colonisation.

Although an attempt to found a colony at Sagadahoc (Maine) also ended in failure, the next attempts at colonisation were more successful. On 24 May 1607 three ships of the London Company of Virginia brought 105 passengers to become settlers in the New World. Virginia survived as a colony, despite extreme weather conditions, periodic attack, disease and other difficulties, to become the most influential American state at the end of the Revolutionary War in 1783. The colony's stability was due in no small part to the fact that it fostered a farming economy, rather than being solely dependent on trade.

John Smith, the first President of Virginia, asked the London Company of Virginia to send him 'good labourers and mechanical men', not merchants and tradesmen.[6] Brogan makes further explanation of the longer-term stability of the English settlements, particularly Virginia, by reference to the territorial and dynastic autonomy of England during the American colonial period.[7] At this time, England, through its island position and lack of dynastic and territorial claims, did not become embroiled in the costly conflicts of continental Europe. Neither was it as susceptible to attack as some of its European neighbours, being virtually able to surround itself with the Royal Navy. By the American colonial period, moreover, the English had both the will and the motivation to survive in the New World.

The composition of Virginia's population was another key factor promoting stability and hence survival. Whereas other colonies initially took their population primarily from one sector of society, whether convicts or 'undesirables' or soldiers, Virginia found popularity with a broad section of English society. In particular, the emerging artisan and tenant class came in great numbers, frustrated by the Enclosure Act and medieval land-holding laws. The rich came to make investments in manufacturing, or to search for the Northwest Passage to the East which they still believed to exist.

John Donne's 'valiant youths rusting and hurtful by lack of employment' were encouraged to go to Virginia for fear that they would destabilise England.[8] For all, however, who wished to raise – or con-solidate – their place in society, land was the biggest attraction. The coincidence of the late Elizabethan period's inflation with the popula-tion boom of the seventeenth century had put such pressure on land resources that aristocrats and labourers alike were clamouring for land. 'In Virginia land free and labour scarce; in England land scarce and labour plenty' was a slogan with wide appeal.[9]

The first leaders of Virginia were autocratic. Smith himself ruled the colony harshly, threatening to starve anyone who refused to work. From the colony's earliest days the tension between co-operation and the seeking of individual gain was high. At first mutineers were ex-ecuted; later they were sent for trial in England.

It was, however, due to Smith's firm governance that the colony sur-vived 'Indian' attacks of 1622 and 1644, as the colonists were not trained soldiers. It was the third and final President, Sandys (in 1624 the Lon-don Company of Virginia was deprived of its charter and the colony reverted to royal control), whose works were to be of lasting signifi-cance.[10] Sandys institutionalised the 'headright' system of land distri-bution. He made sure that each settler was allocated 50 acres of land, along with another 50 acres for each of his dependants. This meant that possession of land became regarded as a right, not as a privilege.

Although Sandys, like his predecessors, was an autocrat, he recog-nised that private land-owners did not readily take to autocratic govern-ance. He made no attempt, therefore, to suppress the establishment of an elected assembly which met periodically to debate and take action upon the affairs of the colony. This assembly, the Virginia House of Burgesses, was made illegal when the colony came under royal con-trol, but by the mid-1630s it was, nevertheless, meeting annually and legislating with the knowledge of the King. The assembly assumed high levels of authority: even by 1635 it was bold enough to remove the Governor of Virginia from office.

On a local level, representative government was more difficult. Hungry for land, Virginians neglected the English model of settlement, the village, and spaced themselves out on their large farms. Their desire for economic independence could only be achieved through physical independence, it seemed.

> This Liberty of taking up Land and the Ambition each Man had of being Lord of a vast, tho' unimproved territory . . . has made the Country fall . . . to this Day they have not any one place of Cohabi-tation among them, that may reasonably bear the Name of a Town.[11]

The slow growth of towns stunted the growth of corporate political activity. Instead of local assemblies, loosely organised – and elite-dominated – counties became the machinery of local government. Each county boasted a court, composed of a sheriff and justices of the peace, along with their staff. The court was an administrative as well as a judicial body; it oversaw elections and the collection of taxes, and held a general peace-keeping responsibility. The counties were rarely democratic and the Governor was responsible for appointing both the sheriff and the judges.

In seventeenth-century terms, however, and after the overpopulated counties of England, consolidation of authority in a relatively small area of land with few inhabitants made the Virginian county system a model of unprecedented representative government. It was also an opportunity for the development of individualism and economic growth.

This model quickly spread in Maryland, the colony adjoining Virginia. Maryland was the first English colony in North America to experience proprietary government. As proprietor, Lord Baltimore intended to model his governance on the English village system, and so gave some 60 large 'manors' to prominent Roman Catholic settlers.[12] Maryland was never attractive as a religious haven, however, and Roman Catholic immigration soon dwindled. The incoming population – mainly Protestants – were unwilling to place themselves under the authority of Roman Catholic 'lords of the manor', however tolerant, and demanded farms of their own.[13] As large numbers of settlers became 'freemen' (landowners) they also demanded an elected assembly. So the new Roman Catholic aristocracy envisaged by Baltimore, along with the last vestiges of feudalism in what was to become the USA, quietly died. In 1635 the Maryland Assembly asserted the right to legislate and, as the village became rarer in Maryland and farms started to play a central economic roll in the region, the Virginian county system of local government became more popular. This was to become the model of local government throughout the South.

Six hundred miles to the north of Virginia new settlement produced the Dominion of New England, a group of colonies that introduced remarkably different political structures into North America, and whose subsequent influence was just as great. The celebrated voyage of the *Mayflower* bringing the separatist 'Pilgrims' ended on 16 December 1620 at Plymouth, just to the north of the recognised boundaries of Virginia.

So, the 'Pilgrim Fathers' began a system of land organisation which reflected their religious beliefs, for it was settled along religious, rather than commercial, principles. The settlement group had been together

12 years as refugees in Leiden (Holland), and so was already shaped by several years of sustained resistance. The group brought a collective and coherent culture which it was determined to preserve.

The 'separatists', as the first 'Pilgrims' had become known in England, were originally part of the mainstream Protestant impetus of the English Reformation. As they were thwarted in their attempts to 'purify' the Church of England, small groups of them established separatist churches of their own, concentrated in Central and Eastern England. An emphasis was placed on the sermon as a means of demonstrating that each person was responsible for their own salvation. The reverence for the sermon was transferred to New England 'secular' culture in the form of respect for public oratory and willingness to attend and participate in public meetings. Sermons stressed the conversion experience and its value as a symbol of a new beginning. Themes of individualism and 'starting over' brought an awareness of individual responsibility and integrity. This community too, albeit for fundamentally different reasons, stressed the themes of individualism and participatory decision-making.

Although the Puritan settlers who followed the original Pilgrims were not separatists (indeed, they remained in contact with the Church of England and became separated from it mainly through geographical distance) they also shared some of these values. Unsure of their legal standing, and conscious that among the *Mayflower* passengers they were in a minority, the Pilgrims drew up a compact to conform to a 'civil body politic'.

This followed the principle already learned by Smith in Virginia: political survival in harsh conditions was only possible with the consent of the governed.[14] This principle was copied by almost all of the groups setting up new settlements in North America.

The constitutions of New Plymouth colony (New Plymouth was later absorbed into Massachusetts) and of Massachusetts were also derived from the Mayflower Compact. These constitutions allowed for the election of a Governor, who would then choose his own council, and, in an unprecedented move towards representative government, the Governor was to be elected (or re-elected) on an annual basis.

In granting the Massachusetts Company a charter with an element of self-rule, Parliament had envisaged authority remaining in the hands of an elite. The Governor of Massachusetts, John Winthrop, and his council willingly adhered to this principle, believing that an excess of democracy was harmful, and that authority was best concentrated in the hands of an educated minority. As Winthrop himself expressed it, 'the best part is always the least and of that best part the wiser is always the lesser'.[15] So, only the small number of freemen met together to discuss matters and to elect the Governor.

Puritan government, however, involved striking a delicate balance between the freemen and the Governor and his council. Against the elitist belief of prominent Puritans was a popular demand for representative and democratic government. Although Winthrop took pains to ensure that the bulk of authority lay with the Governor, this 'enlightened despotism' soon dissipated. Puritanism, as many have suggested, contained the seeds of destruction for its own authoritarian governments, because it laid an inordinate emphasis on the liberty and responsibility of the individual.

As settlers applied for freeman status in their hundreds, therefore, the system of a freeman's council proved inoperable. Although Winthrop made sure that citizenship was confined to 'visible saints', that is, those who were church members, it became necessary to elect deputies who would represent the whole body of freemen at the assembly. In 1634 a representative assembly met for the first time, in Boston, with full authority to legislate while, at the same time, the posts of General Court deputies became elective.

The General Court itself gradually took on the character of the English Parliament; in 1644 it was divided into two houses, the Magistrates and the Deputies, with the consent of both needed to enact legislation.[16] After 1641 the courts used a written set of laws, the 'Body of Liberties', rather than adhering to Winthrop's desire for an organic law based on precedent decision. These laws formally repudiated feudalism.[17]

Local government in New England differed from that in Virginia and Maryland in being organised around the township rather than the county. Since the purpose of emigrating to the New World was to live in closer accordance with God's will, the Puritans were anxious to live in close proximity to the church, and so tended to live in community, rather than apart. This allowed for greater political organisation and, indeed, greater democracy. Consequently, one finds records of all freemen having some 'liberties to vote in things of weightie trust and concernment'.[18] In 1647 the law in Massachusetts was changed to extend the local franchise to all males over the age of 23, whether or not they were 'visible saints'. Given, therefore, that the vast majority of Massachusetts men in the colonial period were church members, it is fair to say that almost any man could vote, gain town office and serve on juries if he set his mind to it. This was a remarkably democratic government for its period of history.

Rigid intolerance encouraged dissenting Puritan groups to leave Massachusetts and follow the example of their forefathers in founding their own settlements. The colony of Rhode Island was granted a charter in 1644, having been founded by two banished exiles from Massachusetts, Roger Williams and Anne Hutchinson. Its charter provided for freedom of conscience and complete separation of church and state. New Hampshire, too, was founded by religious exiles in 1638.[19]

For the most part, however, new colonies were founded in New England to satisfy the demand for fresh economic opportunity. Connecticut was settled with much the same intolerant constitution as Massachusetts. New Haven (absorbed into Connecticut in 1662) was slightly stricter than Massachusetts. Land-hunger appears to be the motivation behind these settlements. 'Sure there were other and better things than the People of God came hither than for the best spot of ground, the richest soil?' questioned a bewildered preacher.[20] In all the New England colonies the settlers preferred their economic unit to be the family; communal land-holding proved unprofitable. For those living on the Eastern seaboard trade was lucrative. New England was rich in fishing and fur, and plentiful timber made sturdy ships for overseas trade. Geographically, New England enjoyed a strategic position for trade, being easily accessible for both European and Southern American ships.

So, by the mid-seventeenth century, characteristics of individualism, economic opportunism and free trade, the separation of church and state, and an unusually developed level of democracy were already established. So too was the multicultural character of the new colonies, although colonists included groups who had settled in the same parts of the continent for religious, or other shared cultural, reasons.

While these early colonists shared many links with England, during the English Civil War (1648–60) emigration was halted, and the relationship between England and the 'English' American colonies grew more distant. New England was forced to draw on its own resources for defence, and by 1643 four New England colonies ('radical' Rhode Island was barred) had come together in a loose federation called the 'New England Confederation'.[21] This alliance eventually disintegrated in the face of internal disagreement, but while it held together it successfully defended the colonies in King Philip's War (1675–76).

The method of colonisation which followed the Restoration in England had more in common with the organisation of the Portuguese American colonies than with either Virginia or New England. Rather than setting up joint-stock companies, King Charles II was anxious to give proprietorships to wealthy men. In return, these men would then supervise the settlement of large tracts of land. He was anxious to utilise the colonies for the best possible economic gain. In the same way that his father had awarded Maryland to Lord Baltimore, the King awarded New York to his brother the Duke of York (later to become James II) in 1664. Although the New Netherlands (as the region was then known) was under Dutch occupation, the Dutch resistance was weak, the settlement being merely a small group of fur-trading stations, rather than an established agrarian society. Since there was little prospect of Dutch attack, James was able to adopt a policy of toleration in New York. Inhabitants were permitted to retain their Calvinist religion, their estates and their commercial practices. These tolerant policies were not as influential in the foundation of colonial North America as they might have been: settlement in New York was very slow until the eighteenth century. Again, the manorial system of land management was short-lived, in this case due to the vast availability of land to whoever wanted it.

As proprietor, James also introduced a coherent set of laws and system of courts with jury-trial to enforce them, together with a certain amount of self-government. Nevertheless, his authority was never in doubt; James banned an elected assembly until 1683, and gave the colony to the Crown when he acceded the throne two years later, at the same time rescinding the Charter of Liberties legislation which had recently been passed.[22]

As a gift of his own, James passed the southern part of New York to two friends, Lord Berkeley and George Carteret. Divided in 1674, the tract of land (known as New Jersey) was settled on its western side by English Quakers, and on its eastern side by immigrants from New England, as well as Baptists from England. The prospects of religious freedom and an elected legislature were attractive after the rigidity of the established Congregationalist Church in New England. The attraction waned somewhat when eastern New Jersey was bought by a group of Quaker businessmen in 1682, but the fear of religious domination passed when New Jersey was restored to royal control in 1702.[23]

Simultaneous with the settlement of New York and New Jersey was the colonisation of land south of the Chesapeake. In 1663 and 1665 King Charles II drew up charters which gave Carolina to a group of eight proprietors. The government and social structure of Carolina was intensely planned. In addition to the royal charters, one of the proprietors and his adviser, the philosopher John Locke, wrote the 'Fundamental Constitutions' which allowed for a hierarchical society with a sub-class of white 'leet-men', black slavery and religious toleration.

Despite these apparent differences, in practice the colony quickly became similar to New York in that it was governed by an appointed Governor and council and an elected assembly. That is, until its diverse economy split Carolina into two colonies by 1712. Peopled by land-hungry immigrants from Virginia, the north of Carolina, on the one hand, became a tobacco-growing economy. On the other hand, the south was settled by displaced planters from Barbados, who joined together with settlers from England to grow rice and indigo as staples, and to establish trade with the Indians.

A more successful attempt at organising a colony was made by the wealthy Quaker, William Penn, who, in 1681, was granted an expanse of land to the east of New York. Lacking a coastline, the founders of Pennsylvania were forced to concentrate on developing an agrarian economy rather than relying on low-investment inter-colony and foreign trade. Penn did buy the former Swedish colonies along the Delaware River in 1682, but they remained separate from the rest of Pennsylvania, and in 1703 became an official colony with an autonomous assembly.[24] Intensive marketing of Pennsylvania among the countries of Europe had yielded a return of 8,000 colonists by 1685. They came mainly from Britain, Ireland, Holland and the German Palatinate, attracted by religious tolerance and the prospect of popular rule. This last was a central tenet of Quakerism, a denomination which rejected outward vestiges of authority and ritual.

Ironically, popular rule was attenuated when Penn, needing the backing of wealthy Quakers, sought to place authority in the hands of the Quaker minority. The planned 'Frame of Government' for Pennsylvania went ahead, but authority was given not to the elected assembly but to the appointed Governor and his council.

The early history of each of these colonies did not always conform to the expectations of their founders, but once again we see the same characteristics of individualism, democracy, economic opportunism (and so on) represented. Interestingly, to these we can see added a new tendency toward religious tolerance, whether for religious or secular reasons.

A similar story is found when one looks at the early history of Georgia. This was also a colony planned by its founders as an idealistic and philanthropic venture, although to the British government it was a strategic defence against the 'Indians' and Spanish-held Florida. In 1732 it was given to a wealthy philanthropist whose committee of proprietors hoped to provide a refuge where debtors could re-start their lives. Slavery was banned (along with rum) and, in an attempt to ensure equitable land distribution, settlers were barred from holding more than

500 acres of land. These high aspirations were held in balance with the aim, and the need, to make Georgia economically viable. The two proved incompatible: few immigrants were attracted to the policies of the proprietors (by the late stage of 1760 its population was only 6,000) and those who did settle – a diverse mixture of English, Scots and Protestant groups from Switzerland and Germany – found it difficult to make a living.[25]

By 1760 all attempts at idealism had been abandoned; land was cultivated on a large scale for rice and indigo, and thousands of Africans were imported to work as slaves. The emergence of large plantations was a pattern reflected all over the Southern colonies, from Virginia to Georgia, and the diverse economy envisaged by many colony founders never materialised. Although the Carolinas dabbled first in the fur trade and later in other commodities, they and the other Southern colonies were drawn to tobacco as a staple cash crop. Labour costs were low, land abundant and markets available (for example, the 1707 Act of Union had made Scotland a large market).

Initially Maryland and Virginia had preferred the use of indentured servants to slaves, but this trend soon reversed itself. In 1680 Virginia had 3,000 slaves and 15,000 indentured servants; by 1715 there were 23,000 slaves and 4,600 indentured servants. At the time of the Revolutionary War there were about 120,000 slaves in Virginia and 57,000 in South Carolina.[26] Growing cash crops was successful: by 1700 production of tobacco brought in £28 million a year, and by 1760 that figure had risen to £80 million a year (a massive 70 per cent of this was grown in Virginia).[27]

Tobacco prices were always unstable, due to economic dependence on a Europe intermittently at war. Southern plantation owners were usually in debt to Britain. Tobacco also quickly exhausted the soil, which led to wheat being produced in Virginia after 1740. Wheat was easier to grow, but brought a lower price.

In general, those freemen who were not plantation owners were small-scale farmers. The only manufacturing was that of pig- and bar-iron. While Baltimore emerged as a thriving centre, other towns remained 'rural' in character. The abundance of unskilled slave labour dissuaded innovation and the agricultural economy was successful enough that by 1760 most farmers were sending a significant percentage of their produce to market.

The economies of the Northern colonies were more diverse. New England exported meat and fish products; its fishing industry was worth £150,000 a year and its whaling industry £50,000 a year. By contrast,

New York concentrated on wheat, while Pennsylvania and New Jersey exported a wide range of wheat products. Commercial activity was an important source of income and offset debts incurred through importing luxury goods. Boston and New York's merchants became carriers for other colonies, and established a reputation as ship-builders in both North America and Europe.

Economic differences led to the differential use of slave labour, and so the differential distribution of the black population. For example, the percentage of blacks in New England remained around 2 per cent over a period of one hundred years in which the percentage of blacks in the Chesapeake leaped from 4 per cent to 39 per cent, and the percentage in the Lower South from 2 per cent to 41 per cent.[28]

Despite the economic diversity, 85 per cent of freemen remained involved in agriculture and much manufacturing took place on a very small scale. New England, in particular, imported goods of a higher value than it exported. It is estimated that while GNP rose at 3.2 per cent for British North America, representing a real per capita growth rate of 0.6 per cent (twice that of Great Britain), New England was the poorest region.[29] There, each white man had a net worth of £33, while the comparative figures for the Middle Colonies and the Lower South are £51 and £132 respectively.[30]

The manner in which slavery developed was closely related to these regional economies. Never homogenous, the institution of slavery and the development of black culture also differed according to geographical region and demographic factors. In the English-American colonies, in the seventeenth and early eighteenth centuries, the numbers of people being held in slavery were relatively small. Throughout the colonial period the proportion of slaves in New England never exceeded 10 per cent (except in Rhode Island where up to 15 per cent were slaves). Since plantations were not a part of the New England economy, the slaves worked on smaller farms, alongside the white indentured servants.

A small number of slaves also held jobs in the emerging Northern industries, particularly in Pennsylvania.[31] In southern New England and New York there were immigrant farmers from the West Indies who aspired to large agricultural farms and, in the manner of their ex-neighbours in Barbados, built mansions and collected slaves more as status symbols than as labourers. In their wills slaves were listed alongside the luxury items rather than the farm tools.[32]

Slaves in the Northern towns, like the black people in the countryside, lived in close proximity to the white population. Using this proximity to identify opportunities for themselves (for example, in the big trading companies), slaves, although not free, gradually absorbed the European culture of whites, their language and their religion.

By the mid-eighteenth century, slaves, were in greater demand. Where black people had once been brought to Boston or New York by the half dozen, now they were imported by the hundred, or more. In 1732 New England began to import directly from Africa, rather than participating in the infamous triangular trade with the West Indies. By 1760 black people working as slaves made up 75 per cent of Pennsylvania's servant population.

The new black immigration had a major impact on black culture in the Northern colonies. No longer living in such close proximity to whites, the black population developed its own distinct culture, drawing on the narratives of the newly arrived immigrants, which re-evoked the memories of older blacks. Where the first generation of slaves, the 'creole', had once absorbed the European culture of their white masters, they now absorbed the culture of their fellow slaves. This new group of slaves found it less necessary to seek out ways of co-existence with the whites.

A significant development in this relationship between the black and white populations occurred in the mid-eighteenth century, when plantation owners in the Chesapeake area became increasingly wealthy with the success of the tobacco economy. Anxious to consolidate their self-sufficiency, they increased their numbers of slaves extravagantly. Where they had once been unskilled field labourers, many slaves were now expected to fill semi-skilled and skilled artisanal positions on the plantation. Where plantation owners had once been distant figures to slaves, and perhaps non-resident, now they took their plantations seriously, establishing daily contact with their slaves.

Despite the decrease in slave autonomy which was produced by the expansion of the plantation, slave communities were strengthened. With the knowledge that their labour was valuable, slaves no longer lived in the same fear. This development hastened the growth of the creole culture, meaning that newly arrived immigrants from Africa did not have the same cultural impact that they did on Northern slaves.

Slaves did not, however, receive greater status, and there remained large numbers of non-land-holding whites who were available to do similar jobs, and to work as overseers of slaves. The primary consequence of this development was that blacks were brought into even closer proximity to whites, encouraging a distinctly African-American culture, rather than one which was mainly African.

In Georgia and the Carolinas the first black slaves came with their 'masters' from the West Indies, where they had learned English and adopted aspects of European culture. Once they arrived on continental North America, moreover, these whites were reliant on blacks. Black people from West Africa were more familiar than whites with the harsh, humid climate found in this area, and were in a position to advise on methods of survival and production. 'Master' and slave were often forced to work side by side in the field or the workshop, so facilitating a further transfer of culture between the two races. Whites were also dependent on blacks to help them defend themselves against the 'Indians' to the West, and French and Spanish to the South.

It was in this region, however, that black people retained a distinctly African culture for the longest period of time. Their harsh environment conquered, whites merged their farms into large plantations in order to produce the staple crops of rice and indigo which were needed for an export economy. Indentured servants were too scarce and too expensive to use as labour; instead, hundreds of black people were imported every year, directly from Africa, to work as slaves. By 1750 South Carolina had more than three black people for every white person, and Georgia, relieved of its charter's ban on slavery, had several counties with black majorities.[33]

So, black American culture did not develop in a uniform manner. To give an example, those who were personal slaves to their 'masters' often acquired discarded European clothes and, less consciously perhaps, European tastes. In the 1770s Charleston Grand Jury recorded that '[the] Law for preventing the excessive and costly Apparel of Negroes and other slaves in this province (especially in Charles Town) [is] not being put into Force'.[34] Interaction could be even more direct: the treatment of the illegitimate offspring of white men and their black female slaves was ambivalent. Sometimes these children were shunned by both races. At least some, however, received more status than had black slaves and some were granted their freedom.

The vast majority of slaves in the Southern colonies were, however, held on large plantations in the countryside. Many of these people had the minimum of contact with whites and, despite the atrocious conditions under which they laboured, many also gained an unprecedented degree of autonomy from their 'masters', perhaps due to the need to grow their own food.

Far from desiring greater integration with the white society, this part of the black population developed a culture which drew heavily on its African origins. At the time of the Revolutionary War many of these black people still spoke African languages, gave their children African names and adhered to African religions.

Despite all this regional variation among both whites and blacks, between 1660 and 1760 the British colonies in North America developed many similarities. With a population growth rate of $2\frac{1}{2}$ per cent per annum (80 per cent of whites were native born; 20 per cent were immigrants), on average women in New England had two more children than European Protestant women. The new generations were healthy, reflecting the relatively high levels of nutrition in North America compared to Europe. For instance, early seventeenth-century North American males were, on average, three to three-and-a-half inches taller than their European contemporaries.[35]

From 1713 onwards, this 'booming' population led to a rapid spread of settlement up to Maine and down to Georgia. The American population was mobile, and inter-colony migration was fairly common in general. For example, in New England – where this pattern was most advanced – between 1660 and 1710, 209 new townships (four a year) were established.[36]

The gradual, partial urbanisation of the colonies was accompanied by the formation of trading centres and a professional class, although Boston, New York and Philadelphia remained the largest towns in the colonial period. Up to half the population in some of these towns worked in the service sector, in professions such as law and medicine, and in transport and commerce. These developments ran alongside the emergence of a more ranked society; by 1740 a distinct social elite had emerged throughout the colonies.[37] Below this elite was a group composed of less successful professionals, artisans, traders and yeoman farmers. Importantly, for our purpose here, most of these people shared the same culture as the elite.

There is little evidence of a permanent 'underclass' in colonial society, but there were slaves. The indentured servant worked only long enough to earn capital for investment. Convicts, imported in their thousands from the UK in the early eighteenth century, also only worked long enough to reclaim their freedom.

Despite this illusion of prosperity and social opportunity, in 1760 slaves constituted 20 per cent of the colonial population.[38] The majority still lived in the South, where the numbers of whites and blacks were roughly equal. But regional demographic variations were already apparent: in the Chesapeake region, for example, there was approximately one black for every white, whereas in New England whites outnumbered blacks by about thirty-five to one.[39] This polarisation on racial grounds was made more acute as the colonies gradually became even more exploitative in their treatment of slaves. In 1776, shortly before the American Revolution, all slavery was legally defined as a 'life-time' condition. The illusion of the 'first Americans' (anyway a problematical term) as freedom-loving liberal democrats is somewhat tarnished when one notes that, while slavery was institutionalised in several areas of the world at this time, only in North America was it used so extensively.

The social characteristics which differentiated late colonial North America from the rest of the world seem to have had a deep psychological impact on its citizens, and so on its society. Bolstered by its unusually large number of 'independent' people, social behaviour became extremely individualistic. There was a concentration on the potential of the individual and many shunned government 'interference' in tasks they could do themselves. Yet, rather than keeping wealth within the narrow boundaries of 'privacy', North Americans invested in their churches, schools, roads and other community structures, seeing development in these areas as a reflection of their own status.

Other social characteristics were more localised. Although the sense of radical, experimental living soon faded amongst the small communities in New England, this region's culture remained distinct from the other colonies. Immigrants to New England usually came as part of a larger social group, at least as part of a family, and there were even complete English villages which re-planted themselves in the colony. As a result, there were proportionately more women in this region: whereas men outnumbered women by at least six to one in mid-seventeenth-century Maryland and Virginia, in New England the corresponding figure was only two to one.[40] Family structure was more stable, and the family was the greatest source of authority.

In the Middle Colonies (New York, New Jersey and Delaware) the society was less homogenous throughout the colonial period. The Governor of New York reported in 1687 that,

> Here bee not many of the Church of England, [and] few Roman Catholicks, [but] abundance of Quakers – preachers, men and women, especially singing Quakers, ranting Quakers, Sabbatarians, Anti-sabbatarians, some Anabaptists, some Independents, some Jews; in short, of all sorts of opinions there are some, and the most part of none at all.[41]

This religious diversity was a reflection of national or ethnic diversity, as it is, in part, in the contemporary USA. The colonial population had its origins in the Netherlands, the French Huguenot departments, the German principalities, Brazil, Africa, Sweden, Scotland, and in the other colonies, in addition, of course, to England. Most of the national or ethnic groups stayed together, and expressed a commitment to their culture. Tensions between them rose, so that by 1700 conflicts were common, especially in New York City, where the English and French exercised political control, despite the numerical superiority of the Dutch. For example, the tensions around the ethnopolitical struggle known as 'Leisler's Rebellion' in New York City in 1689 were only diffused in 1710 by a coalition council composed of both English and Dutch members.[42]

The Southern colonies of pre-Revolutionary North America had a very different social climate. A significant proportion of their population was denied freedom, not only the slaves: throughout the seventeenth century there was a continuous flow of immigrants into Virginia and Maryland, who were committed to indentured servitude. These were people who, unable to afford their passage, agreed to give their labour without reward for a set period – usually about four years – after which they would be given their freedom, and perhaps a piece of land. There was also a flow of about 50,000 English convicts into this region, much to the consternation of the Virginia House of Burgesses, which in 1670 wrote of 'the danger which apparently threatens us from the barbarous designes and felonious practices of such wicked villaines'.[43]

Unmarried males composed a majority of the population, and many succumbed to the unfamiliar malarial diseases. It was commonplace for at least one parent to die before a child reached adulthood, and many children found themselves living with families not biologically their own. These children faced a far more uncertain future than their Northern contemporaries, as there was no family property or dowry to inherit. It has been suggested that the need for security through kinship is the basis of the emphasis on the extended family which is found in some areas of the Southern United States.[44]

Further south, in the Carolinas and Georgia, the population was even more ethnically diverse. Unlike the immediate Chesapeake area and New England, most of the white population was not of English origin. In North Carolina there was a large number of Protestant refugees from all over mainland Western Europe: Baptists, Mennonites, Anabaptists. These small, isolated farming communities spent most of the colonial period struggling to survive as tobacco-growers and cattle-raisers. Attacks from the neighbouring Tuscarora tribes were always imminent.[45] During 1711–13 many North Carolinian settlements were almost destroyed by Tuscarorians. In South Carolina, the small but more stable community of Charlestown looked to Barbados, where many of its settlers and slaves originated, rather than the mainland colonies. Here, too, life remained harsh throughout the colonial period; in the early years of the eighteenth century, traders sent caravans on gruelling year-long journeys to trade furs with the Chickasaw tribes along the Mississippi River. Many of these traders, spending most of their lives in Native American society, became acclimatised to its lifestyles. These *'coureurs de bois'* were violent and feared by the settlers.

Despite the 'wildness' of some of its inhabitants, this area was not 'freer' than those further North: in 1703 Charlestown had slightly more than 7,000 inhabitants, only 3,600 of whom were free whites. The remaining 3,400 people were bound in indentured servitude or slavery, the latter being both slave and Indian. Those under the authority of the free whites suffered harsh punishment for real, likely or imagined misdemeanours, and their 'masters' lived in constant fear of uprising.

On the colonial peripheries there was no structured society. Life was harsh, a bitter struggle for survival, and most people, even those from the most genteel of lifestyles, eventually succumbed to a violent way of life. Earliest accounts of brutality focus on the 'Indian Wars'. In the seventeenth century the Governor and councils of New England colonies paid their settlers a bounty of about £50 for every 'Indian' scalp: whether it was taken from man, woman or child made no difference. As late as 1761, the Governor of South Carolina wrote that, 'We now have the pleasure, Sir, to fatten our dogs with their (Cherokee) carcasses and to display their scalps neatly ornamented on top of our bastions'.[46]

Those who escaped the experience of the frequent 'Indian Wars' were exposed to violence and brutality in other ways. For instance, one of the most popular literary genres throughout the colonial period was the 'captivity narrative'. This was often a pamphlet or small book which gave a detailed account of someone's experience while being held captive by Indians. Pored over, rather than avoided, these narratives brought the fears and perverse excitement of the periphery, or frontier, to all settlements in British North America. It reinforced the view that this was the edge of civilisation, where the European codes of behaviour did not apply. The same savagery was gradually transposed into the treatment of slaves.

Although slavery, by definition, is always a brutal institution, the treatment of the first slaves in British North America was by no means as savage as it later became. Only towards the end of the seventeenth century did extreme brutality become widespread. There is, perhaps, a relationship between the fear felt by free whites of becoming a minority in a, still new, unstable society and the constant fear of 'Indian' attack. That is, the culture of pre-Revolutionary America had already taken on an unusually violent and lawless character, accompanied by an individualistic rejection of previously acknowledged norms of behaviour. Other factors compounded this: the social and political disorder of the periphery was often simply a more explicit version of the thread of civil disorder running throughout colonial society. Many settlers had come to the New World with the express purpose of rejecting the civil society of their homeland. Having rejected the norms of society once, they were not averse to doing so again, were the opportunity to arise. Across the colonies, small discontented groups sprang up, which decided to set up new societies. This phenomenon began to occur soon after the first settlement. To give an example, in 1635 Roger Williams – on his expulsion from the Commonwealth of Massachusetts – set up a town, Providence, in Rhode Island, in which he and his followers sought to live out the purity they believed the mainstream Puritan churches had forsaken. By the end of the century it was Pennsylvania which had become the focus of many mystical, messianistic and pietistic sects, seeking perfection by alienation from mainstream society. The more extreme and mystical of these sects usually died out within one, or perhaps two, generations, but a nucleus of supporters sometimes remained. By 1750, for example, there were more than 60 established German, or 'plain Dutch' (a distortion of 'Deutsch') sects.[47]

Although this tendency to reject the established order ran throughout colonial society, there was a simultaneous move to consolidate existing socio-political structures. Many analysts of the Revolutionary War of 1776–83 have commented on the extraordinary strength of these structures, given the relatively short time they had been in existence, and have cited them as an impetus for the War to throw off British authority.

By 1750, therefore, each colony was governed by an elite group, whose membership was usually composed of professional, sometimes wealthy, white freemen. Whether they governed through elective assembly, or through council, the elite was accepted by the main body of the population. With such an unprecedented proportion of the population bearing the franchise for so long, the assemblies were extremely representative. As a consequence, they were able to resolve conflicts and to absorb new population groups.[48]

By the Revolutionary War, effective and accepted political structures of this sort had been in place for at least a generation. Election was regarded as the basis of acquiring political authority and civil disturbances were rare.

During the later eighteenth century the wealth of the colonies began to increase and self-sufficiency began to be expressed politically: the English North American colonies developed strong bases of indigenous authority and distanced these from the Crown. The outbreak of the English Civil War in 1642 had provided an opportunity for the American assemblies to assume aspects of royal authority, so that, until the English Restoration in 1660, only Virginia had a royal Governor, other Governors being elected by North American freemen. Even after 1660, the provincial assemblies retained more powers of patronage than the Crown's appointees. They, along with aldermen, judges and clergymen, constituted a strong corporate opposition to the royal Governors, and were usually the successful party in Crown–colonist disputes.

The English Crown never took responsibility for establishing sociopolitical order in the new settlements, and in the English colonies these provincial assemblies were instrumental in establishing order. The Massachusetts assembly required each town to send 40 delegates to its sittings; this was a means of incorporating the new regions into the existing order. Of course, the application of this practice was never uniform but, nevertheless, the consolidation of socio-political order in the peripheries was never in serious doubt.

The English colonists in North America also distanced themselves from the spiritual authority of the established Church. In this they were dissimilar to, for example, the settlers in Portuguese Brazil who were not dissenting refugees from the established (Roman Catholic) Church in Portugal, unlike up to 75 per cent of the English colonists in 1776 who were dissenters from the Church of England.[49] In the English colonies, local democratic tendencies had undermined this strand of authority, and even members of the established Anglican Church no longer saw the King as a spiritual authority, particularly after the turbulent Civil War years of the mid-seventeenth century, and the continued rule of 'popish' Stuart Kings.[50]

CONCLUSION TO HISTORICAL REVIEW

Consequently, by the mid- to late eighteenth century, the political, cultural, economic and religious foundations for the American Revolution had been established. The next stage of the analysis must be to identify some of these characteristics of early American political culture, which had come into existence prior to the Revolution. The experience of Revolution, and the foundation of the USA, brought these aspects of colonial society into the core of the earliest US political culture, simply because the new state was formed by participants in this culture.

Politically, some aspects of the culture of US state-formation are well-known today, for example through the Constitution. These tend to be the aspects of early US political culture which stress liberal democratic institutions and personal freedom, and, alongside the social mobility and free-market economy of the early USA, afford what most modern US citizens would see as an attractive picture of stability, freedom, democracy, the rule of law and the possibility for social and economic advancement.

Other aspects which we have seen were also part of the early American state are, perhaps, less well-known. These include a stress on extreme individualism and a disregard for social norms, a tendency towards lawlessness and a disrespect for authority. There was already a tendency towards religious and social experimentation, towards violence and exploitation, and towards ethnic and national separatism, and racism. These characteristics are no less part of the 'initial state' of the USA than are those giving a more attractive picture.

This definition of primary characteristics may be employed to evaluate contemporary trends in the USA. As already suggested, if these trends are similar to those aspects of American political culture and social development which one may identify in this way, then it is possible that they will prove more enduring in the future than those unrelated to what might be seen as underlying trends in US political development, deriving from the circumstances of state-formation. First, however, a simple test will help to ensure that this is not a futile exercise. If the theory that 'initial states', or formative periods of political development, play a continuing role in structuring political history is correct, then the characteristics identified as aspects of the 'initial state' of the USA should be visible in contemporary America.

AMERICAN STATE-FORMATION AND THE CONTEMPORARY USA

The violence and lawlessness of colonial American society and regional variations (for instance, between New England and the South) had transformed the European societies from which colonial communities had sprung into distinctively American cultures. Other characteristics, such as religious experimentation and the rejection of authority in favour of a libertarian individualism, enhanced the heterogeneous character of the USA.

In the economic sphere, growth and opportunity characterised the early American experience, as did a resistance to regulation and a desire to seek new markets. In this area, too, individualism (in the form of economic individualism) prevailed. Interestingly, it has been observed by other scholars that liberalism is the archetypal American political ideology, while economic expansionism and territorial settlement within North America plainly proved key characteristics of the USA.

These characteristics can also be seen to relate to the imperial model of the USA proposed in Chapter 1. It is interesting to note that imperial aspirations were expressed in the early stages of state-formation by such leading figures of the early American state as Washington and Madison. Washington described the USA as 'a rising empire' as early as 1783 and Madison, the so-called 'father of the US Constitution', stated that the new state was to be an 'extended republic' becoming 'one great, respectable, and flourishing empire'. Jefferson also wanted to establish an 'American empire'.[51] While Schlesinger has suggested that these references employ 'empire' in a distinctively eighteenth-century fashion, meaning little more than 'large state', this is open to doubt given the classical education, and so Greek and Roman precedents, upon which eighteenth-century anglophone 'gentlemen' drew.[52] As Agnew has pointed out, the USA rapidly adopted a 'national policy of continental conquest settlement and exploitation'.[53] This is more consistent with an intention to emulate the empires of Alexander or Augustus than to enlarge the existing settler communities alone. Consequently, it may be that the imperial character of the United States is among its initial traits and this, linked to the stimuli of individualism, a dislike of restriction, an urge to economic expansionism and a willingness to use violence, alongside a tendency to exploitation, can be seen as a volatile mixture.

All of these characteristics of American society and politics are still well-known to us at the end of the twentieth century. Levels of lawlessness far exceed those of European states, while an unwillingness to surrender the 'right' to private gun-ownership suggests a preparedness for violence. Cultural attitudes to violence are infamously attested both by media reports and by US popular literature and films. Extreme individualism and religious experimentation are still highly visible aspects of US society and economic liberalism has been extensively demonstrated by studies of both the internal domestic economy of the USA and its foreign trade.

It may be possible, therefore, to recognise all of the most distinctive traits of early America in the contemporary USA. This conclusion enables us to recognise the importance of the study of early political history in understanding contemporary international affairs, and also alerts us to the possibility that one may define characteristics specific to individual states which may continue to be exhibited by them in the future. Such a conclusion does not exclude, however, the possibility that other forms of patterning, such as long-term cyclical change, might not override this heterogeneous pattern of development: we must recall the possibility that processes of change may be hierarchically structured.

IMPLICATIONS FOR THE TWENTY-FIRST CENTURY

If the detailed study of 'initial states', or formative stages, in the political history of the Americas can produce, even in outline, a reasonably accurate understanding of the political cultures of the modern states of the continent, then it is logical to suppose that these characteristics might persist into the next century. If so, then the process of amplification presumed by the theory might intensify the characteristics identified, rather than erode them over time.

This is not to suggest that there can be no development which alters the fundamental characteristics of a state's political culture. This is not the case, because one could envisage cultural change as achievable both from within aspects of existing political cultures and through more wide-ranging changes in beliefs, attitudes, aspirations and values transforming long-held characteristics. While such change is plainly neither easily achieved nor capable of simple imposition from outside the society in question, it remains a significant possibility.

Such a widespread cultural change might derive from the trends discussed in Chapter 2, if it were not that US political culture, and US culture in general, were being transmitted to the newly emergent ethnic and cultural groups, such as the Hispanic population of the USA. As we saw in that chapter, both Asian- and Hispanic-Americans have remained culturally distinct within the US population, but partial assimilation has occurred. So this change, in itself, is unlikely to be sufficient to alter the political culture of the USA, except in regard to ethnic relations and regional separatism, as already mentioned. This brings us to the question of what the implication of these trends is for the central theme of this book, supposing that no resolution of this sort is found. It is, therefore, worth examining the consequences of these trends for the future political history of the USA, as was attempted in Chapters 2 and 3.

The amplification of the trends implied by our definition of the 'initial state' of the USA suggests that, rather than decrease in significance, they may result in an increase of violence, lawlessness, the carrying of private weapons, economic competition and economic liberalism, and a rejection of both government and other forms of authority. The breakdown of legal and other restriction, combined with an intensified heterogeneity in society, might also be expected on these grounds, as could intensified regionalism.

As such, many of these trends are precisely those highlighted in Chapter 2 of this book. There, they were documented on empirical grounds as characteristics of the contemporary USA which seem to constitute trends of increasing seriousness or extent. Worryingly, they could also be a recipe for state-collapse, if this is seen as potentially deriving from an intensified divergence of interests, aims, beliefs or values. It seems clear that, far from allaying our fears for the future stability of the USA, a long-term perspective on US political culture suggests that these trends represent a serious danger to the future success, and even political survival, of the USA.

5 The Global Context of American Instability

The preceding chapters have sought to show that the USA is a territorial empire and that it is, at present, exhibiting tendencies which suggest that it is politically unstable. The argument that this is the case has rested on the view that the US empire is within, rather than outside, the USA as it exists today. That is, the modern state is itself 'imperial' in both formation and structure and this is accompanied by economic and cultural imperialism within its borders. Instability, therefore, derives from the probable accentuation of existing trends toward cultural change, social polarisation, economic decline and demographic shifts. This is unlikely to lead to the rapid demise of the USA as a state, although it may be expected that a greater emphasis on regional separatism will emerge in the twenty-first century.

Instead of state-collapse, the next decades may bring a growth in political instability undermining the ability of the USA to compete with its external rivals or to halt internal trends, let alone to reverse them. Such high-stress circumstances, no less than the early stages of state-collapse itself, may in turn promote the emergence of more authoritarian government, if social psychological studies of the effects of stress on human social groups are to be credited.

This pattern is supported by the significance of the initial state of state-formation which has been demonstrated in Chapter 4 and by trends already more advanced in Canada, discussed in Chapter 3. The first chapter set out some general arguments, based on studies of global change overall, to suggest that US decline is occurring and that the USA has already lost 'superpower' status in international affairs.

All of these threads of argument lead to the conclusion that in the next half-century the USA will exhibit an increased level of internal destabilisation, arguably accompanied by more draconian measures designed to combat this, and a parallel reduction of the international role of the USA. On this basis alone, one would expect the USA to be a 'middle-ranking' (but not lesser) 'power' in the mid-twenty-first century.

Such a conclusion is based on grounds distinct from those used by Paul Kennedy or Edward Luttwak; neither is this simply a reflex of the authors' political preconceptions about the USA. For instance, it does not derive from a predisposition towards a 'declinist' view due to a concealed political programme or Marxist ideology. Simply, it is a re-reading of twentieth-century American political history in a long-term context and an evaluation of its short-term (historically-speaking) implications for the future of the USA.

An interpretation of this kind, which sees US pre-eminence ending as the 'American century' draws to a close, inevitably raises interesting questions regarding the global position of the USA today and its prospects in the international arena in the next half-century. This has, of course, been a major theme in the work of other scholars, especially Professors Nye and Kennedy.

This chapter will go beyond the simple conclusion that the USA is declining from 'superpower' status, to examine its prospects in terms of the global politics of the early twenty-first century. It will be argued that an examination of the international context supports the view that, in the early twenty-first century, the USA will be neither a 'dwarf' (a 'lesser power' in the international arena) nor a 'giant' (a 'superpower'), but one of a series of approximately 'equal' states in a more equally balanced inter-state system without any pre-eminent 'superpower'. First, however, it is necessary to achieve two preliminaries to such a discussion: the presentation of a brief outline of US foreign affairs since the end of the Cold War and the evaluation of the, currently fashionable, view held by scholars of international relations: that the inter-state system itself is 'withering away' in the face of growing transnationalism and an increase in the role played by international institutions.

Following these analyses, we shall present a review of the relative role of the USA in the present and near-future, in relation to its major 'competitors' in global politics: the European states, China and Japan. The exclusion of the former Soviet Union (FSU) from this list reflects the view that the FSU is unlikely – barring unforeseen changes – to become the leading actor in world politics prior to 2040, even if its current low point proves to be a transient, or at least short-lived, phase in its history.

Finally, we shall be returning to the Americas, to evaluate the place of the USA in the continental inter-state system. Together, these examinations will provide the basis for a conclusion drawing together the results of this review to assess the prospects, both for the USA and for the emergence of what Kennedy would call 'great powers' in the next century.[1]

THE USA IN CONTEMPORARY INTERNATIONAL POLITICS

The USA entered the post-Cold War world as the principal victor of the Cold War.[2] Economically and militarily, it was by far the leading 'great power' when the Soviet Union fragmented into the post-Soviet republics. In cultural terms, its influence was widely felt through telecommunications, film, media and material aspects of Americanisation.[3] Its liberal-democratic ideology seemed, to many, to be the only viable alternative for the political systems of the future: 'the end of history', no less.[4]

Yet one may note that strains in America's relationships within the international system were almost immediately visible. Although the first post-Cold War test of the USA – the Gulf War of 1991 – was accompanied by a surprisingly 'painless' victory for the Americans and the Allied forces, the optimism expressed in George Bush's 'New World Order' speech in March 1992 was not to last.[5] Within the following years, the USA became embroiled in the disastrous expedition to Somalia, and its 'undisputed hegemony' was soon damaged by, for example, its apparent inability to secure a settlement of either the Kurdish or Bosnian crises.[6]

In Asia, increasingly the focus of post-Cold War US foreign policy, North Korea openly flaunted the might of the Americans especially and, in Europe, Germany and the United Kingdom proved more 'independently-minded' than might have been envisaged in 1991. For both sides, by 1995, the US:UK 'special relationship' seemed diminished, if not extinct: the United Kingdom was no longer the USA's most obedient foreign ally in Europe; the period of 'post-Suez' shock to British self-esteem was over.[7]

Economically, the USA was faring little better by 1995.[8] A 'jobless recovery' may have been under way, but this was accompanied by growing popular dissatisfaction with Clinton's Democrats, as seen in the Republican success in the Congressional elections of that year.[9] US business continued to lose ground internationally, compared to its 1945 position, in relation to both its Asian and, to a lesser extent, European competitors.[10] National debt, often cited by scholars of international relations (who, as we have seen, tend to emphasise economic factors when discussing change) as a crucial factor in the post-World War II loss of 'great power' status by Britain and France, became a major factor in American politics.[11]

Not all was bleak, however: the USA retrieved the situation in Haiti and defence cuts were less extreme than might have been anticipated at the end of the Cold War.[12] US nuclear supremacy was ensured, making America almost certainly secure from total defeat in large-scale conventional war.[13] This was, itself, a 'hollow' aspect of victory, for no longer were there any potential opponents whose conventional or nuclear forces might constitute a serious threat of this sort.[14]

While US cultural importance was unaffected by all of this, nationalist and cultural-revivalist movements ensured that the new nations of the former Soviet Union did not adopt exclusively US-style culture and values. Although Americanisation now spread to those regions previously Soviet-dominated, the cultural sphere remained alone as an area of dramatic US advance as a 'global hegemon' in the post-Cold War period.[15]

The position of the USA as a political and military 'hegemon' among the Western Allies was now, itself, in severe doubt, as European states reasserted common bonds and political identity through the European Union and the Western European Alliance. In NATO, the European partners also adopted a more assertive role, while retaining a strong preference for a US involvement.[16] Requests for a reform of the United Nations and Bretton Woods institutions again served to challenge the 'hegemonic interests' of the USA.[17]

In this situation – of very rapid 'relative decline' from 'lone superpower' to disputed hegemon – where does the USA's proposed 'New World Order' fit in? This will be the next topic of discussion.

'THE NEW WORLD ORDER' AND THE END OF US GLOBAL LEADERSHIP

When Bush announced the 'New World Order' in March 1992, he claimed that, 'The United States has a burden to bear ... we are the leaders and we must continue to lead'.[18] Although, as the Gulf War ended, US global leadership may have seemed assured, this has plainly not occurred. Bush and his government wanted to reorder the international system so as to promote the non-violent settlement of disputes and to guarantee the security of all nations, large and small.[19] This dream was at once shattered by the Kurdish crisis following the Gulf War itself, while US interventions (especially that in Somalia) pushed it further into the realms of unrealised historical ideals. Despite this, Cheney may have been correct when he claimed that the Gulf War was 'a defining event in the new post-Cold War world'.[20] In retrospect it, rather than the economic heights of the 1950s–60s, can be said to show the apex of US pre-eminence.

Neither was the US government unaware of the difficulties which faced it in the post-Cold War world.[21] The need to place more emphasis on conventional forces and to prepare for 'mid-intensity conflict' such as might derive from 'Third-World challengers' to US interests were clearly recognised policy aims.[22]

Yet the delusion that high-technology weapons systems (such as 'smart bombs') were responsible for the rapid US-led victory in the Gulf has clouded this clarity of perception.[23] So, too, has the even more striking delusion that the development of Strategic Defence Initiative was principally responsible for the end of the Cold War and the fall of the Soviet empire.[24]

What had occurred was the establishment of military forces designed to meet the Soviet threat. Expensive to maintain or to disestablish, these forces continued to be a major drain on US resources.[25] Yet they remain the main surviving vestige beyond the cultural sphere of the lost status of the USA in the post-World War II world. Consequently, to cut these forces is to slide further into 'decline' in both military and psychological terms; to refurbish them probably also enhances the process of decline in economic terms.

The utility of either strategy depends almost entirely upon the nature of the threats facing the USA in the next century. These might take contrasting forms. For instance, guerrilla or terrorist campaigns against US interests or inside the USA would require very different responses from those employing medium-scale conventional attack. Nuclear, biological and chemical ('NBC') weapons form another unknown factor: the prospect remains of the terrorist or guerrilla use of these weapons, or their use by state actors challenging the USA in their own regions.[26]

The problem the USA faces in regard to the proliferation of NBC weapons is simple. This seems an unstoppable trend overall and the most likely acquirers of NBC weapons are among those states least amenable to US diplomacy.[27] Worse still, the USA has no ability to control the illegal trade in weapons-grade nuclear material, and the missile sites and missile carriers of the former Soviet Union could be seen as insecure, given the economic crisis in the region.[28] That is, while the passage of fissile material to a hostile state or group is easily conceivable, it is not inconceivable that short- or even medium-range launchers and other delivery systems may be illegally in the hands of hostile groups by the end of the twentieth century, if they are not already.

Such weapons do not constitute a direct threat to US territory, but could prove decisive in a medium-scale conflict between the USA and a Third-World state, in the context of extensive media coverage and hostile public opinion. It may be an accurate calculation that the USA is unready to bear the burden of high levels of casualties among its military personnel to win a distant, medium-sized war. If so, the military options open to the USA would be greatly limited by the proliferation of such weapons. The extent of the Iraqi NBC arsenal, as established following the victory in the Gulf War, should alert us to the scale of this problem.

US 'impermeability' from 'low-technology' attack is not as certain as might be supposed. A terrorist attack on mainland USA could employ either conventional or NBC weapons. While this would certainly have a negligible military effect, and probably be inconceivable as an overall plan of attack, the psychological effect of such an attack could be devastating.[29]

Again, the principal problem is not of US interests being directly threatened, but of the realisation by many states, and other interest groups, of the substantial 'powerlessness' of the USA.

'Tooled up' to fight a war which took on a fundamentally different character from that which was expected by military strategists, it has failed to 'win' the 'peace' that followed by imposing its 'New World Order' through persuasion or coercion. So, the failure of the 'New World Order' – the culmination of many US 'international institutionalist' liberal projects in the nineteenth and twentieth centuries – has indicated the emptiness of the 'US hegemony' which some scholars, especially Professor Nye, claim still exists. Rather than date the decline of US 'hegemony' from the 1970s or 1980s, it is this 'definitive event' – the US-led victory in the Gulf War – which, it is argued here, both saw the apex of US global dominance and was followed by its swift 'relative decline' in the 1990s.

TRANSNATIONALISM AND THE EROSION OF SOVEREIGNTY

Although this is not the place for a lengthy discussion of current debates in international relations theory concerning the declining importance of states in international affairs in relation to transnational actors and exchanges, the relevance of such exchanges must be considered here.[30] The growth of global communications in the twentieth century, of global economic and cultural institutions and the rapid rise in the number of international institutions of all sorts, has led to a large number of transactions and contacts which take little account of state sovereignty.

While some scholars have seen this as a direct threat to the continued existence of the state, this does not seem a plausible development within the next half-century. States continue to play a central role in international affairs, whether in military or diplomatic terms, and are frequently represented within the international institutions which might be argued to have taken over some of their functions.

Such transnational exchanges and non-state actors have, however, both increased the permeability of the state and intensified international linkages. Consequently, the domestic politics of any state, including the USA, is now closely linked to international politics, and vice versa.[31]

The interpretation put on these linkages, here, is that they are likely to increase the significance of US domestic crisis for international politics. They are also likely to make economic growth less closely tied to the political status of states than has seemed to be the case since World War II.

Transnationalism is, therefore, potentially important to the future prospects of the USA in that domestic change and international affairs are closely interconnected. Economic recovery is unlikely to lead to national recovery on its own.

THE RETURN OF EUROPE

Robert Gilpin has suggested that the start of US decline should be dated to October 1979 when the US government requested the support of Germany for the dollar and this was refused.[32] Others have noted that Germany has increasingly come to represent a major threat to US economic interests through the 1980s and 1990s and that the economy of the EU states together, including Germany, is now larger than that of the USA.[33] Given Germany's low level of foreign commitments and still relatively low level of security spending in relation to the USA, it may be possible for this situation to be maintained at least in the next few decades.[34] If so, then the maintenance of the NATO alliance is crucial to German national interests as it reduces the need for German security spending in the unstable international atmosphere of the post-Cold War world. Germany's geographical position, close to many former Soviet states and so potentially under threat from the results of post-Soviet regional instability, makes this an especially important question for the Germans.

Shifts in the character of military forces, especially to more small-scale and highly mobile specialist forces with fewer but far more highly trained military personnel, have deep-seated implications for European security.[35] Changes in the force-structures of the UK, France and Germany may permit greater flexibility in post-Cold War security for these countries, than that open to the USA without major military restructuring. In both military and economic terms, therefore, the US role in Europe may be replaced by a greater European contribution both to NATO and to European security in general.[36] In NATO, it must be remembered that Europeans already provide 80 per cent of the tanks and combat aircraft and 90 per cent of the workforce, so that any increase in the European component of NATO would shift the emphasis of the alliance firmly towards being European-centred.[37] If, as analysts have recently suggested, NATO assumes an increasingly important role in international security outside Europe, and if the EU becomes one of the principal trading blocs in the international economy, then the European role in international affairs will become much more significant than during the Cold War.

The 'long peace' in Europe seems set to be maintained into the twenty-first century in relation to the internal security of the principal European actors: Germany, France and the UK.[38] The absence of external threat is also likely to be maintained, especially in relation to the UK and France, and probably both Germany and Italy. For the latter states, however, Eastern Europe and North Africa may, respectively, prove potential sources of new security threats, as these have been currently perceived by NATO itself.[39] Given the rise of the Western European Union (WEU) and increased German defence spending in NATO, these two processes may become more enhanced in the twenty-first century.

The US role in Europe has, of course, already been declining since the end of the Cold War. Increasingly isolationist pressures in the USA, combined with economic decline and the collapse of the Soviet threat, has made the costs of maintaining a substantial, but militarily ill-placed, force in Europe outweigh the benefits. If Europeans increasingly look to their own security and the European Union increasingly forms a competitive and closed market in relation to the USA, then the US role will almost certainly continue to diminish. The resurgence of European culture and cultural initiatives by the European Union are likely to further undermine American cultural inputs, although it is extremely unlikely that these will cease to be a significant part of European cultural life in the next few decades.

It is interesting, also, that a trend towards a retreat from Europe may already be visible in the USA, where recent survey suggests that 90 per cent of Americans would be prepared to renounce a leading global role to achieve economic growth and where cultural links with Europe seems to be declining.[40] At the same time, European spending on European security has, for example, surged ahead of that by Americans. Even as the Cold War came to an end in the 1980s, there is some evidence that the Europeans were building their own security system, less dependent on that of the USA.[41]

Although much attention has concentrated on Germany[42] in view of the over-riding significance assigned by many analysts to economic factors, other European states have also been changing their relationship to the USA. In the 1980s, for the first time since the early 1960s, both the British and the French engaged in successful military operations outside Europe.[43] These operations showed at least some degree of military and political independence from the USA, as have British and French domestic and foreign policies in the late 1980s and early 1990s.

Such independent-mindedness can be seen to have been enhanced by the end of the Cold War and reflected in the weakening of the 'special relationship' in the 1990s. So, in the same way as Germany has been prepared to return to the global stage in the post-Cold War period, it may be that other European states will follow suit. Interestingly, the existing evidence suggests that they are likely to do so in different sectors of international affairs, where they already hold relative advantages.

One might expect Britain and France to play a greater diplomatic and military role in the post-Cold War period, and Germany and Italy to play a greater economic role than during the Cold War. Some co-ordination and mutual benefit gained from membership of the EU may enhance the relative competitiveness of these European states compared to the USA within those sectors of the international system in which they already have a role.

For example, the strengths of Britain's unconventional and specialist military forces and its considerable anti-terrorist expertise may be a significant advantage in the new period of international security.[44] The relatively small nuclear deterrents held by Britain and France may also be more cost-effective given the lack of potential aggressors with larger nuclear forces in the post-Cold War international system.[45] In such a situation, more than a minimum nuclear deterrent may be a very expensive 'luxury' for the USA.

Likewise, European awareness of American decline is liable to promote an even greater sense of independence and a reassertion of a global role by pre-1939 'great powers' in Europe. While there is no likelihood of a return to inter-War roles by Britain, France and Germany, it seems probable that these major European actors will be more significant in the world politics of the next half-century than they were during the half-century from 1945 to 1995. In this sense, it is likely that the early twenty-first century will see a 'return of Europe' to international affairs.[46]

Interestingly, in his most recent book Professor Kennedy himself has come to regard the EU as a potential 'great power' of the twenty-first century.[47] While his conclusions in this respect rest on some different grounds, and place a greater importance on EU unity than seems legitimate in the face of strong nationalist traditions and global trends towards political fragmentation, it may be significant that he has reached a similar interpretation of the rise of this region in the post-Cold War world.[48]

Kennedy's original view was, of course, that Japan would be the most probable successor to the global role of the USA.[49] This is, therefore, an appropriate context in which to discuss the changing role of Japan.

THE ASIAN CHALLENGE TO US GLOBAL DOMINANCE

One need hardly state that, after its disastrous defeat in World War II, Japan is now a leading economic actor in contemporary international affairs. In the heyday of US economic might, the 1950s and 1960s, nowhere was more certainly part of the US overseas 'informal empire' than Japan. The effect of this was to lead to the foundation of a new Japanese state after World War II based on the US in both constitutional and economic terms.[50]

Some aspects of this new state are especially notable here. First, the importance, from 1947 onwards, placed on economic reconstruction was to lead to the transformation of the Japanese economy.[51] This involved harsh economic measures which resulted in the 'normalisation' of the Japanese economy by 1954–55.[52] Second, one might note the importance of the Constitution of 6 March 1946, which (under Article 9) forbade Japan to have military forces and to engage in warfare.[53] Following the peace treaty of 1951–52, Japan was re-admitted into the mainstream of international affairs, and in the 1950s an economic boom took place which was assisted by restrictions on imports and accompanied by a somewhat less America-dominated foreign policy.[54]

By 1960, a new Japan had emerged.[55] This had a flourishing economy,

Western-style government and full political independence from the USA, but was strongly pacifist both in its constitution and the overall orientation of its population. Towards the end of the decade, in 1968, Japan's economy came to exceed that of West Germany, then the world's third largest economic unit.[56]

Trade competition and US rapprochement with China led to a rift in US:Japanese relations in the early 1970s, and by the end of the decade there were attempts to establish links between the Japanese economy and those of the Soviet Union and China.[57] The place of Japan among Western capitalist democracies was not, however, in jeopardy, but US politicians began to fear Japanese competition in the international economy.[58] Despite these changes, Japan still retained a low level of defence spending and upheld the constitutional commitment to capitalism.[59]

In the 1980s and early 1990s, US fears intensified. Japanese investment in the USA became a significant issue in US domestic politics while, as Garnham has pointed out, of the world-wide top 100 firms in 1989, 53 were Japanese in contrast to 35 American.[60] Of the top five firms world-wide, all were Japanese.[61]

By focusing on economic factors, the USA came to regard Japan as a key competitor in world affairs. Increasing Japanese independence and suggestions of US decline, notably those of Kennedy himself, intensified this fear. Cultural distance and perhaps even wartime memories added to this perception of Japan's imminent rise to global dominance.

Interestingly, by focusing on the alternative variable of military strength, one would get a contrasting image of Japan's international role. In military terms, Japan is highly dependent on Western security guarantees and is not a major military actor in international affairs.[62] If it was not for the security framework provided by the USA and its Western allies, Japan would easily be open to pressure from its neighbours, were these states to wish to intervene in its affairs.

So, in economic terms, Japan might seem to be a competitor for global dominance, but this is not the case in military terms. Nor, if only for linguistic reasons, is it likely that Japanese culture will assume the same global role in the twenty-first century as did American culture in the later twentieth century, and it is highly unlikely that, outside of the economic sector, Japan will export its political or other ideologies and belief systems to the rest of the world.[63]

Given Japan's post-War pacifist heritage and the low incentive for it to play an increased military role in international affairs, it is also extremely unlikely that Japan will change its role in international security in a fundamental fashion. While it may be increasingly drawn into UN peace-keeping and other collective activities, there is no indication that it will develop an expansionist foreign policy, nor that it would profit by doing so.[64]

While in the view of those scholars and others who would place primacy on economic factors, Japan would seem poised to dominate the twenty-first century, this does not in fact seem likely. To make such a claim is to disregard Japanese values, culture, historical experience and post-War politics. All but a small minority of modern Japanese do not seek a new Japanese empire in the Pacific and the national experience of attempts at regional dominance has been both painful and deep-seated.[65] Military adventure might threaten Japanese economic success and incur significant psychological and political costs.

Consequently, while Japan is likely to remain an important actor in international politics in the twenty-first century, its role is likely to be as a leading economic player rather than a major diplomatic or military force. Nor should we assume that Japanese economic growth, or even the maintenance of its current regional economic dominance, will continue unhindered into the twenty-first century. With increased regional competition from Southeast Asia and China, it is very unlikely that Japan will maintain its current share of world markets.[66] If the EU and NAFTA develop more protectionist economic policies in the face of East Asian economic growth, then the Japanese share of the American and European markets may fall drastically.[67]

That is, neither in military nor in economic terms, is there strong evidence that Japan will assume the role in the early twenty-first century which the USA played in the late twentieth century. It is far more likely to be one of a group of regional 'middle-rank' actors with large economies and, perhaps, isolationist cultural attitudes stretching from Korea to Indonesia.

The principal alternative rival for dominance in the Pacific to both Japan and the USA is China.[68] With its huge internal market and apparent military strength, the position of China in relation to the USA is arguably reminiscent of that of the USA in relation to Britain in 1900. Yet, as we shall see, it is likely that China will also fail to become the dominant international actor even in the Pacific region, let alone globally.

CHINA AND THE US ROLE IN THE PACIFIC

In highlighting the potential of Japan as a challenger to the USA as a global 'superpower', there is the danger of overlooking China. The rapid development of the Chinese economy towards technological capitalism, and its incomparable human resources in terms of population size and degree of popular mobilisation, make it potentially a major economic and political actor.[69] In the military sphere, China has both nuclear weapons and Inter-Continental Ballistic Missiles and is capable of delivering these in a strategic nuclear conflict, combined with large numbers of tanks and combat aircraft.[70]

Yet, as we have seen when discussing Europe, superiority in numbers of nuclear devices and 'heavy' conventional weapons, such as tanks, may be far less significant in the early twenty-first century than during the Cold War. The same problems of regional competition as noted for Japan can also be identified as potential constraints on the Chinese economy.

There are also severe problems relating to Chinese society and politics, which are likely to become aggravated rather than alleviated in the next generation. Socially, capitalism has promoted a greater sense of individualism and this has been combined with increased openness to Western cultural values.[71] These changes exist in a constant tension with the domestic political system and continued communist dominance of the state.[72]

Neither are demographic factors likely to operate entirely to the advantage of the Chinese government. Current restrictions on the birth rate have led to a gender imbalance in the infant population, with the number of infant boys far outnumbering girls.[73] This may cause social problems of an, as yet, unknown scale in the coming generation. Such a gender imbalance is also likely to have the positive effect of slowing the rate of population growth and so promoting economic development, but as economic development may well, itself, be having the effect of promoting Western values, this may also be a destabilising factor.

During the 1970s and 1980s, cultural exchanges and commerce between China and the West grew very rapidly.[74] For example, between 1979 and 1986, 35,000 Chinese students studied in the USA and 4,000 Americans taught in China.[75] Such a transfer has significant cultural, as well as educational, effects, especially in the urban areas. The Westernisation of young Chinese is the most striking aspect of this, again being promoted rather than restrained by economic freedom.[76]

Other factors are also playing a significant role. The very rapid rise of the Christian Church in the 1980s and 1990s has attracted considerable interest both from scholars and from the Western media. Exact figures for the number of believers are unclear, but plainly a Christian minority exists in contemporary China and this is growing.[77] It is especially significant, in political terms, that the most intensively Christianised segment of the population is also that most open to Western education and the new market economy.[78] That is, this part of the population is likely to become more important as China develops a Western-style economy and Westernisation spreads more widely.

Consequently, deep-seated changes have affected young Chinese in the 1980s and 1990s and are likely to be seen in the early part of the twenty-first century. The political and social implications of religious, cultural and demographic change are uncertain, but it is clear that the most highly-educated and probably economically-dominant group in twenty-first-century China is likely to be very far removed from the Cultural Revolution, and even from Marxism, in terms of its beliefs, values, culture and outlook. It is very difficult to see how this can fail to bring about fundamental changes in Chinese politics, although, as the Tiananmen Square incident showed, the Communist party is unlikely to surrender political leadership in the face of localised protest.[79]

The probability of political change and democratic reform through the emergence of a new generation in the Chinese leadership is high, but this is unlikely to take place until well into the twenty-first century, although it is possible that reformers will come into prominence before this. It is, therefore, likely that China will see an intensification of tensions between contrasting interest groups.

It may be folly to suppose that the Chinese will make the transition to a post-Marxist state easily. It is worrying in this context that China has been prepared to use harsh measures against both dissidents and neighbouring states.[80] Central Asia may, for example, prove to be an attractive zone for Chinese expansion if population pressure does not decline as expected, but there are only ambiguous indications of expansionist trends in contemporary China.

Likewise, the growth of the Chinese economy may have such disastrous effects for the economy of Southeast Asia and Japan that these states and the economic interests based in them might be expected to fiercely resist any such change. Economic competition can, therefore, be expected to act as a brake on Chinese development while internal tensions may pose significant constraints on an increased global role.

Nor is there much prospect of China being able to export its culture or political ideology in a post-Cold War context. It is very unlikely that one would see Chinese culture assuming the role once held by American culture, even in the Pacific, and a return to communism internationally seems extremely unlikely.

Despite the apparent potential for China to assume the role of a regional hegemon, it is, therefore, implausible that such a role is within its grasp. The collective importance of the Southeast Asian states and Japan may act as a significant bar on this.

OTHER POTENTIAL CHALLENGERS

The same problems that face Japan and China in terms of regional competition and the constraints imposed by their own cultures and political neighbours may be said to apply even more strongly to the Southeast Asian states.[81] This may limit the potential of any one of these states to achieve dominance in the Pacific. Nor is it conceivable that the African states, even South Africa, might become a potential successor to the USA in its global role.[82] African unity seems almost an impossible prospect within the next generation and internal political differences and religious tensions make an Islamic alliance in the Middle East implausible.[83] For example, it seems unlikely that Iran and Saudi Arabia could be brought together within a single federal state or alliance of sufficient coherence as to threaten the dominance of the West in international politics. While the Arab world might constitute a potential source of further conflicts, an Arab contender for global dominance is not a serious prospect.

Neither is Latin America likely to produce a new 'great power' and, for example, Australia is in no position to assert itself as more than a significant regional actor.[84] So, the conclusion of this brief survey must be that there is no clear successor state poised to seize a position of global dominance. Several states – among them Japan, China, Germany, France and the UK – may play a far more significant role in international affairs than at present, but none of them are likely to be able to assert the dominance either in all sectors of the international system or in regional terms. The emergence of regional or global hegemons is, therefore, unlikely.

Consequently, it is possible to propose an alternative model for the development of international affairs in the early twenty-first century in relation to the rise and fall of major states, but not of what Kennedy calls 'great powers'. This is based on the foregoing survey and our assessment of the future prospects for the USA.

A RETURN TO MULTIPOLARITY

In a variety of sectors significant actors seem to be emerging, or have the potential to emerge in the early twenty-first century. It is, however, notable that these are not the same actors in each sector of international affairs. Likewise, major constraints on the dominance of any actor in each sector makes unchallenged supremacy extremely improbable. Nor is regional supremacy likely to emerge from these changes.

Thus, it is possible to envisage a situation of classic state-based multipolarity, rather than (or as well as) the multipolarity of economic blocs sometimes envisaged as likely in the post-Cold War period. In this, there may be a series of major actors, each significant in one or two sectors of the international system. These actors might be expected to include all the present members of the UN Security Council and also Germany and several Southeast Asian states, as well as Japan.[85] Of these, there is no reason to suppose that any would be able to exercise overall dominance or hegemony, but the development of existing links, such as those through the UN, EU, NATO and economic institutions, might promote some degree of international co-operation.

The situation might come, therefore, in some respects to resemble a global version of the 'Concert of Europe' – a state-based multipolar system of approximately equally-matched actors, each with identifiable strengths and weaknesses – and be paralleled by relative international peace. Changes in the character of warfare make world war or global nuclear war very unlikely, and this too might enhance the stability of this new international order.[86]

That is, the end of the Cold War may have brought about a return to circumstances reminiscent of those prevailing in Europe after the Napoleonic War. This is a conclusion similar to that which has been arrived at on different grounds by other scholars, although few have argued for the separation of sectoral dominance and return to prominence of the principal European actors suggested here.

It must be stressed, however, that this model differs from others in taking account of factors other than economic and military aspects alone, in the emphasis placed on the cultural matrix of international politics and in incorporating the view that both the USA and Russia will also be middle-rank actors in this system by the mid-twenty-first century. This model of the emerging post-Cold War international system is also different from the post-Cold War multipolarity which has been envisaged by Waltz and Nye. Both of these scholars have suggested that a new multipolar system will emerge from the competition of major economic blocs, such as the EU and NAFTA. In the view presented here, individual states within these blocs will continue to be key actors in the international system, an interpretation reached not through the imposition of theoretical neo-realism, but by the historical consideration of contemporary change. This brings us to the question of the changed domestic character and international role of the USA.

AN ALTERNATIVE VIEW OF THE USA IN THE TWENTY-FIRST CENTURY

If current trends continue, the USA will not be the pre-eminent economic or military actor in twenty-first-century international affairs. It will not exercise global leadership or hegemony in the West, and possibly not even unchallenged hegemony in the Americas. The programme to establish a 'New World Order' will have failed, if it has not already.

To begin with domestic characteristics, massive cultural and demographic change may lead to a poorly-educated and impoverished, principally Hispanic-American, lower class. This will co-exist with a far smaller group of wealthy and better-educated citizens of different cultural backgrounds, sharing little in common with each other or with the lower class. Crime and lawlessness are likely to increase rather than become more controlled, while the cities may be more disorderly and in steeper economic decline than at present. Social polarisation may lead to increased class tensions and conflict between cultural groups and to more civil disorder. Geographical zoning may reflect social and cultural distinctions and economic differences.

In a situation where economic decline and large-scale unemployment combine with these characteristics and a reduction in the ability of government to control the American population, internal processes of national decline may be highly visible. The Los Angeles riots may give some indication of the form that such tensions might take.

This level of social and economic decay may provide a context for the growth of regionalism and possibly of regional separatism. This may be especially noticeable in those areas where convergence with Latin America, or with what is now Canada, coincide with an erosion of national and cultural differences. If Canada breaks up into regional states, this may lead to an increase in the importance of separatist movements in the USA. Were this to occur, and it is a plausible rather than necessary scenario for the early to mid-twenty-first century, it is possible that potential cleavages might separate California, Texas, Hawaii and possibly even Florida and Alaska from the USA.

The prospect of the political break-up of the USA in the first half of the twenty-first century is much less likely than the intensification of regional differences and social conflicts, although it is not, perhaps, impossible. It does not seem as likely that the USA will fragment rather than that it will be weakened by such changes, in both domestic and global terms. Nor is the collapse of US liberal democracy especially likely. Instead, it is possible to imagine that voters would elect increasingly authoritarian governments and be prepared to accept far harsher economic and other legislation in order to stabilise and attempt to manage such trends, or, alternatively, to see federal government as increasingly irrelevant.

It must be stressed that this interpretation is based on a reading of trends which already exist in the Americas, in the context of contemporary international affairs and long-term aspects of political history. There is, of course, no way in which one can know that these types of change will occur working from such evidence. Neither is there a deterministic law governing change which necessitates such developments. Without a drastic transformation in domestic and international affairs, these or similar changes are, however, those indicated by contemporary trends.

CONCLUSION

This book has attempted to re-read the political history of the New World to produce a new understanding of what America is today, what the distinctive characteristics of American political development are and how its political history is shaped by the past, and to evaluate the prospects for its immediate future. By recognising the USA as a territorial empire, albeit one with benign as much as exploitative aspects, and seeing the Cold War as an inter-imperial conflict, the context of twentieth-century history since 1945 is more clearly comprehensible in terms of world history in general. On this reading America loses its uniqueness in terms of international politics.

By recognising the significance of state-formation, and of culture, in subsequent political history, a logical basis for the projection of trends recognisable in the present can be established. Identifying and defining current trends permits us to use this to re-evaluate potential future developments, with the crucial proviso of the limits of historical predictability.

These approaches, while used to reconsider the question of American decline and the prospects of a 'New World Order' based on US global dominance, might form the basis for studies of other areas and states. They might be employed to examine non-state actors and to enhance our ability at trend analysis in regard to specific themes or issue-areas in international affairs.

By highlighting the dangers facing the USA, we hope to alert American scholars and others to the potential risks which domestic factors pose for the nation. It is important not only for Americans but also, as Susan Strange has pointed out, for the world, that the 'relative decline' of the USA from 'superpower' status is managed as efficiently and responsibly as America managed its role in the Cold War. The extent to which it can preside over its own decline may be a clear indication of the 'greatness' of a nation and will be a measure of the degree to which the USA is still able to live up to the ideals of the Founding Fathers.

Notes

1 The Fall of the American Empire?

1. We use 'America', to refer to the United States of America, as interchangeable with 'the USA' and (as an adjective) 'the US', simply to avoid tedious repetition. By 'the Americas' we mean the entire continent, as geographically defined.

2. What we mean by 'trend analysis' is the chronologically forward projection of current sequences of related or similar events, as applied conventionally in demographic studies and economics. For an interesting discussion of alternative approaches, and the problems of this approach, see the UN's useful book: World Futures Studies Federation, *Reclaiming the Future: a manual on futures studies for African planners*, (London, 1986). Other works on trend analysis are Linda Starke (Ed.), *Vital Signs: The trends that are shaping our future, 1994–1995*, (London, 1994), and Donella H. Meadows, Dennis L. Meadows and Jørgen Randers, *Beyond the Limits: Global collapse or a sustainable future*, (London, 1992). For a theoretical discussion of 'complexity' and international relations see K. R. Dark, *The Waves of Time?* (London, 1996).

3. But note that not all those who write of 'the American Empire' are on the 'Left': for example, Marvin Wolfgang, *The American Empire: Expansion or Contraction*, (Newbury Park, 1988).

4. See the useful discussion in Arthur M. Schlesinger, *The Circles of American History*, (Boston, 1986), pp. 128–155.

5. Notably, of course, Paul M. Kennedy, *The Rise and Fall of the Great Powers: Economic Change and Military Conflict from 1500 to 2000*, (London, 1987).

6. J. O'Connor, *The Fiscal Crisis of the State*, (New York, 1973); J. A. Hobson, *Imperialism: a study*, (London, 1902). For an overview of theories of imperialism see: W. J. Mommsen, *Theories of Imperialism*, (London, 1981), and Wolfgang J. Mommsen and Jurgen Osterhammel (Eds.), *Imperialism and After: Continuities and Discontinuities*, (London, 1985).

7. R. Hilferding, *Das Finanzkapital*, (Vienna, 1910).

8. J. A. Schumpeter, *Imperialism and Social Classes*, (New York, 1951).

9. J. Galtung, 'A Structural Theory of Imperialism', *Journal of Peace Research*, 8, (1971), (pp. 81–117).

10. D. Foeken, 'Explanation for the partition of sub-Saharan Africa 1880–1900', *Tijschtift veer Economische en Social Geografie*, 73, (1982), (pp. 138–148); N. Mansergh, *The Coming of the First World War: A Study in the European Balance 1878–1914*, (London, 1949); A. P. Thornton, *Imperialism in the Twentieth Century*, (London, 1978).

11. R. Robinson, 'Non-European foundations of European imperialism: sketch for a theory of collaboration', in R. Owen and B. Sutcliffe (Eds.), *Studies in the Theory of Imperialism*, (London, 1972), pp. 117–40.

12. G. Lichtheim, *Imperialism*, (Harmondsworth, 1971).
13. Galtung, 'A Structural Theory of Imperialism'.
14. Peter J. Taylor, *Political Geography: World-Economy, Nation-State and Locality*, (3rd Ed., Harlow, 1993); K. Buchanan, *The Geography of Europe*, (Nottingham, 1972).
15. C. C. O'Brien, 'Contemporary Forms of Imperialism', in K. T. Pass and D. C. Hodges (Eds.), *Readings in US Imperialism*, (Boston, 1971).
16. For discussions see: Anthony Breaser, *Marxist Theories of Imperialism*, (1980); Norman Etherington, *Theories of Imperialism: Conquest, War and Capital*, (London, 1984); David F. Healy, *Modern Imperialism*; Richard H. Kroebner and Helmut Dan Schmidt, *Imperialism: the story and significance of a political world, 1840–1960*, (Cambridge, 1964); Tony Smith, *The Pattern of Imperialism*, (Cambridge, 1981).
17. For example, Stephen Hemmingham, *France and the South Pacific: A Contemporary History*, (Sydney, 1992).
18. P. J. Cain and A. G. Hopkins, *British Imperialism: Innovation and Expansion, 1648–1914*, (London, 1993), pp. 161–180.
19. V. I. Lenin, *Imperialism: the highest stage of capitalism*, (New York, 1939).
20. See reference n. 16.
21. For a recent review of the evidence relating to the early Roman empire and its context see: K. Randsborg, *Europe and the Mediterranean in the first Millennium AD*, (Cambridge, 1990).
22. R. Aaron, *The Imperial Republic: the United States and the World 1945–1973*, (Englewood Cliffs, 1974); G. Liska, *Imperial America*, (Baltimore, 1976).
23. J. Gallagher and R. Robinson, 'The Imperialism of Free Trade', *Economic History Review*, 2nd ser. 6, (1953), (pp. 1–15).
24. Arthur M. Schlesinger, *The Cycles of American History*, (London, 1987), pp. 129–162; Klaus Schwabe, 'The Global Role of the United States and its Imperial Consequences, 1898–1973', in Mommsen and Osterhammel (Eds.), *Imperialism and After*.
25. Schwabe, 'The Global Role of the United States'; A. E. Campbell, 'The Paradox of Imperialism: the American Case', in Mommsen and Osterhammel (Eds.), *Imperialism and After*, p. 4, and Tony Smith, 'American Imperialism is Anti-Communism', in Mommsen and Osterhammel (Eds.), *Imperialism and After*, pp. 41–48.
26. W. A. Williams, *The Roots of the Modern American Empire*, (New York, 1969).
27. The following section is based on Emily S. Rosenberg, *Spreading the American Dream: American Economic and Cultural Expansion, 1890–1945*, (New York, 1982), and Thomas G. Patterson and Stephen G. Rabe (Eds.), *Imperial Surge: the United States abroad, the 1890s to the early 1990s*, (Lexington, 1992).
28. Schwabe, 'The Global Role'.
29. *ibid.* p. 18.
30. *ibid.*
31. The principal sources for this account are: Hugh Brogan, *The Pelican History of the United States*, (Harmondsworth, 1986); Robert Gilpin, *The*

Political Economy of International Relations, (Oxford, 1987); Maldwyn Jones, *The Limits of Liberty: American History 1607–1992*, (Oxford, 1994); George B. Tindall and David E. Shi, *America: A Narrative History*, (4th Ed., London, 1994). Other material is referenced in the text.

32. Tindall and Shi, *America: A Narrative History*, p. 221.
33. Jones, *The Limits of Liberty*, p. 103.
34. *ibid.* p. 394.
35. Tindall and Shi, *America: A Narrative History*, p. 573.
36. Brogan, *The Pelican History of the United States*, p. 450.
37. Tindall and Shi, *America: A Narrative History*, p. 586.
38. *ibid.* p. 333.
39. *ibid.* p. 571.
40. *ibid.* p. 574.
41. Christopher Coker, 'Intimations of Mortality?', in Christopher Coker (Ed.), *Shifting into Neutral? Burden Sharing in the Western Alliance in the 1990s*, (London, 1990), p. 28.
42. *ibid.*
43. Among the wide range of general and thematic works on the later twentieth century US economy in its international context see: Nicholas Spulber, *The American Economy* (Cambridge 1995), M. Destler, *American Trade Politics* (2nd Ed.) (Washington 1992), Robert Lawrence and Charles L. Schultze, *An American Trade Strategy: Options for the 1990s* (Washington 1990), Eric Helleiner, *States and the Reemergence of Global Finance: From Bretton Woods to the 1990s* (Ithaca 1994), Robert E. Baldwin, *The Political Economy of U.S. Import Policy* (Cambridge (Mass.) 1985), Robert E. Baldwin (Ed.), *Recent Issues and Initiatives in US Trade* (Cambridge (Mass.) 1984), Martin Feldstein (Ed.), *The American Economy in Transition* (Chicago 1980), Martin Feldstein, 'American Economic Policy and the World Economy', *Foreign Affairs* 63 (1985), 995–1008. Several useful recent papers on the USA in the global economy are reprinted in *International Political Economy* edited by Jeffry A. Frieden and David A. Lake (2nd Ed.) (London 1991): Barry P. Bosworth and Robert Z. Lawrence, 'America in the World Economy', 429–441, Robert Baldwin, 'The New Protectionism: A Response to Shifts in National Economic Power', 362–375, G. K. Helleiner, 'Transnational Enterprises and the New Political Economy of U.S. Trade Policy', 353–361, Edward John Ray, 'Changing Patterns of Protectionism: The Fall in Tariffs and the Rise in Non-Tariff Barriers', 338–352. Also, see: 'A Survey of American Business', *The Economist* 15, page supplement 16–22nd (September 1995).
44. Pierre Martin, 'The Politics of International Structural Change: Aggressive Unilateralism in American Trade Policy', in Richard Stubbs and Geoffrey R. D. Underhill (Eds.), *Political Economy and the Changing Global Order*, (London, 1994), p. 439.
45. Gilpin, *The Political Economy of International Relations*, p. 240.
46. *ibid.* p. 232.
47. *ibid.* p. 243.
48. *ibid.* p. 238.
49. *ibid.* p. 239.
50. *ibid.* p. 249.

51. *ibid.* p. 251.
52. J. Nef, 'The Political Economy of Inter-American Relations: A Structural and Historical Overview', in Stubbs and Underhill (Eds.), *Political Economy and the Changing Global Order,* p. 406.
53. *Americas Review 1993/4,* (13th Ed., 1994), p. 156.
54. *ibid.* p. 159.
55. On Canadian economic history see: R. E. Caves and R. H. Holton, *The Canadian Economy,* (Cambridge (Mass.), 1961), Richard Pomfret, *The Economic Development of Canada,* (Toronto, 1984), William L. Marr and Donald G. Patterson, *Canada: An Economic History,* (Toronto, 1980); there is also a useful overview in: P. J. Cain and A. G. Hopkins, *British Imperialism: Innovation and Expansion 1688–1914,* (London, 1993), pp. 258–273, which also summarises political developments to 1914.
56. *Americas Review 1993/4,* (13th Ed., 1994), p. 160.
57. Stephen E. Ambrose, *Rise to Globalism: American Foreign Policy since 1938,* (Harmondsworth, 1993), p. 369.
58. *Americas Review 1993/4,* (13th Ed., 1994), p. 148
59. For US foreign policy see: Gordon Martel (Ed.), *American Foreign Relations Reconsidered 1890–1993,* (London and New York, 1994), Nigel Bowles, *The Government and Politics of the United States,* (London, 1993), pp. 327–359, Phil Williams, 'Foreign Policy', in *Developments in American Politics,* edited by Gillian Peele, Christopher J. Bailey, Bruce Cain and B. Guy Peters, (London, 1994), pp. 289–310, Stephen E. Ambrose, *Rise to Globalism* (7th Ed., London, 1993), Charles W. Kegley Jr and Eugene R. Wittkopf, *American Foreign Policy: Pattern and Process* (4th Ed., New York, 1991).
60. Ambrose, *Rise to Globalism,* p. 86.
61. Coker, 'Intimations of Mortality?', p. 30.
62. Martin J. Hillenbrand, 'American Perceptions of NATO and the European Community', in Coker (Ed.), *Shifting into Neutral?,* p. 112.
63. Thornton, *Imperialism in the Twentieth Century,* p. 32.
64. Frank W. Peers, 'Tensions over Communications', in Elliot J. Feldman and Neil Nevitte (Eds.), *The Future of North America: Canada, the United States and Quebec Nationalism,* (Cambridge, Mass., 1979), p. 94.
65. *ibid.* p.89.
66. Joel Rosenbloom, 'Response to "Tensions over Communications"', in Feldman and Nevitte (Eds.), *The Future of North America,* p. 107.
67. Michael Kidron and Ronald Segal (Eds.), *The New State of the World Atlas,* (4th Ed., London, 1991), p. 76.
68. Thomas E. Skidmore and Peter H. Smith, *Modern Latin America,* (3rd Ed., New York, 1992).
69. Kidron and Segal (Eds.), *The New State of the World Atlas.*
70. *ibid.* p. 75.
71. *ibid.* p. 142.
72. *ibid.*
73. For the Cold War in the context of inter-imperial conflict see: Morris J. Blachman and Donald J. Puchala, 'When Empires Meet: The Long Peace in Long-Term Perspective', in *The Long Postwar Peace,* edited by Charles

W. Kegley, Jr., (New York, 1991), pp. 177–201.

74. *ibid.* p. 184.

75. Participants ranged from those who strongly resisted any talk of decline (such as Henry R. Nau, *The Myth of America's Decline,* (Oxford, 1990)) to those who saw the case for decline as convincing, such as Coker, 'Intimations of Mortality?', pp. 22–40. Some had already come to the conclusion that the USA was in steep decline even before Kennedy wrote, for example: Terry Boswell and Albert Bergeson (Eds.), *America's Changing Role in the World System,* (New York, 1987). For an overview of the debate and its principal protagonists, see Joseph S. Nye, *Bound to Lead,* (New York, 1991), pp. 1–21. For later views see: Aaron L. Friedberg, 'The End of the Cold War and the Future of American Power', in *The Fall of Great Powers,* edited by Geir Lundestad, (Oslo and Oxford, 1994), pp. 175–96, Paul Joseph, *Peace Politics: The United States Between the Old and New World Orders,* (Philadelphia, 1993), Richard Ned Lebow and Janice G. Stein, *We All Lost the Cold War,* (Princeton, 1994), Richard Maidment and J. A. Thurber (eds), *Politics of Relative Decline,* (Cambridge, 1994), David P. Rapkin, *World Leadership and Hegemony,* (London, 1990), Joseph Hippler, *Pax Americana: Hegemony and Decline,* (Boulder, 1994), Peter Savigear, 'The United States: Superpower in Decline?', in *Dilemmas of World Politics,* edited by John Baylis and N. J. Rengger, (Oxford, 1992), pp. 334–53, Susan Strange, 'The "Fall" of the United States: Peace, Stability, and Legitimacy', in *The Fall of Great Powers,* edited by Geir Lundestad, (Oslo and Oxford, 1994), pp. 197–211.

76. Susan Strange, 'The Persistent Myth of Lost Hegemony', *International Organisation,* (41)4, (1987), (pp. 551–74), and *Casino Capitalism,* (London, 1986), pp. 22–3.

77. David Garnham, 'The United States in Decline?' in Coker (Ed.), *Shifting into Neutral?,* pp. 3–21 (esp. p. 12).

78. Charles W. Kegley., Jr. and Gregory A. Raymond, *A Multipolar Peace? Great-Power Politics in the Twenty-first Century,* (New York, 1994).

79. Strange, 'The "Fall" of the United States', pp. 175–96.

80. *ibid.* p. 207.

81. Joseph S. Nye, *Bound to Lead,* and 'What New World Order?', *Foreign Affairs,* 71, (1992), (pp. 83–96), and 'No, the US isn't in Decline', *New York Times,* 30 October 1990, p. 33. For a review of Nye's arguments, see Paul Kennedy, 'Fin de siècle America', *New York Review of Books,* 28 June 1990, p. 32.

82. Nye, 'What New World Order?' p. 88.

83. Albert Bergesen and Ronald Schoenberg, 'Long Waves of Colonial Expansion and Contraction, 1415–1969', in *Studies of the Modern World-System,* edited by Albert Bergesen, (New York, 1980), pp. 231–277.

84. Peter Taylor, *Political Geography: World-Economy, Nation-State and Locality* (3rd Ed., London, 1993).

85. K. R. Dark, *The Waves of Time,* (London, forthcoming).

86. George Modelski, *Exploring Long Cycles,* (Boulder, 1987), George Modelski, *Long Cycles in World Politics,* (Seattle, 1987), George Modelski

and W. R. Thompson, *Leading Sectors and World Power*, (Columbia, 1995).

87. On the conflict and collapse of empires in the twentieth century, and for its political history overall: J. P. D. Dunbabin, *The Post-Imperial Age*, (London, 1994), J. P. D. Dunbabin, *The Cold-War*, (London, 1994).

2 Domestic Political Instability in North America

1. An honourable exception is Chapter 7 of Joseph S. Nye, *Bound to Lead: The Changing Nature of American Power*, (New York, 1990). An almost diametrically opposite view of the global implications of American domestic 'decline' to that in this book is presented in James Petras and Morris Morley, *Empire or Republic? American Global Power and Domestic Decay*, (New York, 1995). The nearest in approach to the present work is David P. Calleo, 'America's Federal Nation State: a Crisis of Post-imperial Viability?', *Political Studies* XLII, (pp. 16–33).

2. For a discussion of theories of global change, see K. R. Dark, *The Waves of Time*, (forthcoming).

3. The Constitution of the United States, Amendment XXVI, 30 June 1971, in George B. Tindall and David E. Shi, *America: A Narrative History*, (2nd Ed., London, 1989), p. A22.

4. Nicholas J. Rengger, 'Culture, Society and Order in World Politics', in John Baylis and N. J. Rengger (Eds.), *Dilemmas of World Politics: International Issues in a Changing World*, (Oxford, 1992), pp. 88–96.

5. Oran R. Young, 'The Effectiveness of International Institutions: Hard Cases and Critical Variables', in James N. Rosenau and Ernst-Otto Czempiel, *Governance Without Government: Order and Change in World Politics*, (Cambridge, 1992).

6. For the political and social history of the USA see Maldwyn A. Jones, *The Limits of Liberty: American History 1607–1992*, (Oxford, 1995).

7. H. G. Nicholas, *The Nature of American Politics*, (Oxford, 1986), p. 5.

8. Leonard J. Arrington and Davis Bitton, *The Mormon Experience: A History of the Latter Day Saints*, (London, 1979), p. 162.

9. Tindall and Shi, *America: A Narrative History*, pp. 248, 341.

10. Jones, *The Limits of Liberty*, p. 174.

11. 'Brown et al. v. Board of Education of Topeka et al. 17 May 1954', in Clayborne Carson, David Garrow and Gerald Gill (Eds.), *The Eyes on the Prize Civil Rights Reader: Documents, Speeches and First Hand Accounts from the Black Freedom Struggle 1954–1990*, (London, 1991), pp. 64–74.

12. Aldon D. Morris, *The Origins of the Civil Rights Movement: Black Communities Organising for Change*, (London, 1984), p. 17.

13. See, for example, James Deetz, *In Small Things Forgotten*, (Garden City, 1977), John W. Blassingame, *The Slave Community: Plantation Life in the Antebellum South*, (Oxford, 1979), Robert L. Schuyler (Ed.), *Archaeological Perspectives on Ethnicity in America*, (Baywood, 1980).

14. On black Americans and US politics and society see Lee Sigelman and Susan Welch, *Black Americans' Views of Racial Inequality*, (Cambridge, 1994), Paul M. Sniderman, Philip E. Tetlock and Edward G. Carmines (Eds), *Prejudice, Politics, and the American Dream*, (Cambridge, 1995).

15. Arthur Schlesinger, *The Disuniting of America: Reflections on a Multi-Cultural Society*, (London, 1992), p. 24.
16. *ibid.* p. 25.
17. Alexis de Tocqueville, *Democracy in America*, translated by Richard N. Heffner, (New York, 1956), p. 132.
18. *ibid.* p. 138.
19. Tindall and Shi, *America: A Narrative History*, p. 295.
20. Schlesinger, *The Disuniting of America*, p. 30.
21. *ibid.* p. 35.
22. *ibid.*
23. Tindall and Shi, *America: A Narrative History*, p. 574
24. *ibid.* pp. 766–767.
25. Schlesinger, *The Disuniting of America*, p. 39.
26. *ibid.* p. 37.
27. On the 'crisis of identity' in the USA see: Howard Fineman, 'Shifting Racial Lines', *Newsweek*, 10 July 1995, 52–53, Jerry Adler, 'What is an American?', *Newsweek*, 10 July 1995, 30–35, Robert L. Earle and John D. Wirth (Eds), *North American Identities*, (Cambridge, 1995).
28. Schlesinger, *The Disuniting of America*.
29. *ibid.* p. 16.
30. *ibid.* p. 52.
31. On re-segregation see also *The Economist*, 7–13 October 1995, p. 18, which observes that 'America is steadily resegregating' and concludes that 'America is two countries not one. And these are growing apart, not together.'
32. Schlesinger, *The Disuniting of America*, p. 105.
33. *ibid.* p. 113.
34. *ibid.* p. 133.
35. *ibid.*
36. Seymour Martin Lipset, 'Revolution and Counter-Revolution – The United States and Canada', in Thomas Ford (Ed.), *The Revolutionary Theme in Contemporary America*, (Lexington, 1965).
37. Louis Hartz (Ed.), *The Founding of New Societies: Studies in the History of the United States, Latin America, South Africa, Canada and Australia*, (New York, 1964).
38. Robert Finbow, 'Ideology and Institutions in North America', *Canadian Journal of Political Science*, XXVI(4), (1993), (pp. 671–697).
39. Government of Canada, *The History of Canada's Constitutional Development*, (Hull, Que., 1991). See also R. Weaver, *The Collapse of Canada*, (Washington, 1992).
40. Barbara Ryan, *Feminism and the Women's Movement: Dynamics of Change in Social Movements, Ideology and Activism*, (London, 1992), p. 101.
41. *ibid.* p. 68.
42. *ibid.* p. 106.
43. *ibid.* p. 77.
44. Naomi Black, 'Ripples in the Second Wave: Comparing the Contemporary Women's Movement in Canada and the United States', in Constance Backhouse and David Flaherty (Eds), *Challenging Times: The Women's Movement in Canada and the United States*, (Montreal, 1992).

45. P. Resnick, *Towards a Canada–Quebec Union*, (Montreal, 1991), p. 19. Weaver, *The Collapse of Canada*.
46. Statistics Canada, 1991.
47. *Macleans*, 22 April 1991, p. 18.
48. *ibid*.
49. Recently the population of Quebec fell below 25 per cent of the total population of Canada, the psychological 'water-shed' and the basis on which the Charlottetown Consensus on the Constitution granted 25 per cent of House of Commons' seats to Quebec. At the same time, statistics showed that the population of the Western provinces was growing proportionately faster than that of other regions. British Columbia's population, for example, grew by 2.5 per cent in 1994, double the national average of 1.1 per cent. *Globe and Mail*, 7 April 1995, pp. A1, A5.
50. J. L. Finlay and D. N. Sprague, *The Structure of Canadian History*, (Scarborough, Ontario, 1989), p. 102.
51. Gill Rémillard, 'Under What Conditions Could Quebec Sign the Constitution Act?', in Michael Behiels (Ed.), *Quebec since 1945*, (Toronto, 1987), p. 209.
52. 'The Constitution Act 1982, Section 15', in Finlay and Sprague, *The Structure of Canadian History*, p. 553.
53. *ibid*. p. 417.
54. Peter Clancy, 'Native Peoples and Politics in the Northwest Territories', in Alain G. Gagnon and James Bickerton (Eds.), *Canadian Politics: An Introduction to the Discipline*, (Peterborough, Ontario, 1990), p. 559.
55. *ibid*. p. 573.
56. Finlay and Sprague, *The Structure of Canadian History*, p. 178.
57. *ibid*. p. 230.
58. *ibid*. pp. 222–230.
59. *Macleans*, 4 May 1992, p. 16.
60. On changing patterns of migration see: Stephen Castles and Mark J. Miller, *The Age of Migration*, (London, 1993).
61. Andrew Hacker, *U/S: A Statistical Portrait of the American People*, (New York, 1983), p. 45.
62. Kevin Phillips, *The Politics of Rich and Poor*, (New York, 1991), p. 210.
63. William Wilson, *The Truly Disadvantaged: The Inner City, the Underclass and Public Policy*, (London, 1987), pp. 7–8.
64. There are complicated procedures for defining 'North American'. By 2002, cars, for example, will have to have at least 62.5 per cent local content before they can be freely moved between Canada, the United States and Mexico. Richard Buckley (Ed.), *NAFTA and GATT: The Impact of Free Trade – Understanding Global Issues*, (Cheltenham, 1994), p. 4.
65. *ibid*. p. 5.
66. The general rules on services state that the member states have to respect service providers from other NAFTA members by not requiring that they set up local offices. The service providers must also be given both national and most-favoured nation treatment by the host country. Buckley (Ed.), *NAFTA and GATT: The Impact of Free Trade*, p. 4.
67. *The Economist*, 25 February 1995, p. 78.

68. For present links between California and Mexico see: A. F. Lowenthal and K. Burgess (Eds), *The California–Mexico Connection*, (Cambridge, 1993).
69. Sidney Weintraub, 'US–Mexico Free Trade: Implications for the USA', in *Journal of Interamerican Studies and World Affairs*, 34(2), (1992).
70. Buckley (Ed.), *The United States*, p. 9.
71. *ibid.* p. 18.
72. D. Ethier, *Democratic Transition and Consolidation in Southern Europe, Latin America and South East Asia*, (London, 1990).
73. David Hamilton, 'Poverty Is Still With Us – And Worse', in Fred Harris and Roger Wilkins (Eds), *Quiet Riots: Race and Poverty in the United States*, (New York, 1988), p. 37.
74. Tindall and Shi, *America: A Narrative History*, p. 245.
75. Peter Calvert and Susan Calvert, *Latin America in the Twentieth Century*, (London, 1990), p. 85.
76. *ibid.* p. 84.
77. Peter G. Boyle, *American–Soviet Relations: From the Russian Revolution to the Fall of Communism*, (London, 1993), p. 237.
78. Calvert and Calvert, *Latin America in the Twentieth Century*, p. 188.
79. Thomas E. Skidmore and Peter H. Smith, *Modern Latin America*, (3rd Ed., New York, 1992).
80. *ibid.*
81. *Report of the Deutsche Bundesbank for the Year 1991*, (Frankfurt, 1992), pp. 3–7.
82. Boyle, *American–Soviet Relations*, p. 241.
83. Walter Lafeber, *America, Russia, and the Cold War, 1945–1992*, (London, 1993), p. 347.
84. Paul Kennedy, *The Rise and Fall of the Great Powers: Economic Change and Military Conflict 1500–2000*, (London, 1987), p. 554.
85. Lafeber, *America, Russia, and the Cold War*, p. 347.
86. *ibid.* p. 346.
87. *ibid.* pp. 353–354.
88. *ibid.* p. 351.
89. This account is based on David Nye, *Contemporary American Society*, (Arhus, 1990), pp. 45–56, and *The Economist*, 19 October 1991, pp. 56–57, but note that, if oil revenues 'dry up' as suggested then this itself might have significant political and social impacts.
90. Nye, *Contemporary American Society*, pp. 50–59; *The Economist*, 3 April 1993.
91. *The Economist*, 5 December 1992, estimated a 30 per cent population increase by the early twenty-first century, with the number of non-Hispanic Americans outnumbering Black-Americans in twenty years. Stephen Castles and Mark J. Miller, *The Age of Migration*, (London, 1993), pp. 249-51; Jane Jaquette, *The Future of Inter-American Relations* (La Jolla, 1985), p. 3 makes a similar estimate to that reported in *The Economist*. Skidmore and Smith, *Modern Latin America*, p. 379 give an estimate of the Hispanic population of the USA at present.
92. Steffen W. Schmidt, Mack C. Shelley and Barbara A. Bardes, *American Government and Politics Today*, (New York, 1995), pp. 19, 168–171 and 175–77.

93. See references cited in n. 91; *The Economist*, 27 June 1992, p. 57.
94. *ibid.*; Bruce Cain, 'Developments in Racial and Ethnic Politics,' in Gillian Peele, *et al*, *Developments in American Politics* (2nd Ed., London, 1994), pp. 45–66 (44–52); *The Economist*, 8 September 1990. 47.8 per cent California; 23 per cent Texas; 12 per cent Florida in state populations 1980–90. Current figures (*The Economist*, 12 November 1994, p. 58) are that Hispanics comprise 26 per cent of Californians, while Asians comprise 9.5 per cent. ·
95. See references cited in n. 91; *The Economist*, 27 June 1992, p. 57.
96. *The Economist*, 27 June 1992, p. 57.
97. *ibid.* and see references cited in n. 91.
98. Education in the USA is unlikely to rectify this in favour of 'majority culture': for example, see, Christopher Coker, 'Intimations of Mortality?', in Christopher Coker (Ed.), *Shifting into Neutral?*, (London, 1990), pp. 22–40 (p. 26), who states that the general public in the USA exhibit low levels of general education, including the statistic that 60 per cent of Americans never read another book after High School.
99. For the history of Asians in the USA: Bill Ong Hing, *Making and Remaking Asian America Through Immigration Policy 1850–1990*, (Cambridge, 1994).
100. *The Economist*, 20 February 1993, p. 56, and 27 June 1992, p. 58. On cross-border population flows note, Castles and Miller, *The Age of Migration*, pp. 91–2, 95, 170–2, 174, and 249–51.
101. See references cited in n. 91.
102. Note the violent rhetoric, militarism, size and organisation of these groups: for example, *The Economist*, 29 April 1995, pp. 60–61 reports that there are more than 100 such groups, with one group claiming 12,000 members, although lower estimates have been proposed. The leader of this group told journalists that he sees 'warfare, armed rebellion' being 'inevitable'. At least some of these groups have been trained by ex-professional soldiers.
103. Joanne O'Brien and Martin Palmer, *The State of Religion Atlas*, (London, 1993), p. 78.
104. *ibid.*, pp. 78, 124.
105. Cain, 'Developments', p. 51.
106. For the events preceding independence: Roger C. Thompson, *The Pacific Basin since 1945*, (London, 1994), pp. 185, 284.
107. Brian Hocking and Michael Smith, *World Politics: An Introduction to International Relations*, (Hemel Hempstead, 1990), pp. 83–107; Charles W. Kegley and Eugene R. Wittkopf, *World Politics: Trend and Transformation*, (5th Ed., New York, 1995), pp. 176–189.
108. On the importance of the Bretton Woods system to the US, see Coker, 'Intimations', p. 28.
109. Thomas Omestead, 'Selling Off America', pp. 208–19 and Mack Ott, 'Is America Being Sold Out?', pp. 220–29, both in Jeffrey Frieden and David A. Lake (Eds.), *International Political Economy*, (2nd Ed., London, 1991).
110. David Garnham, 'The United States in Decline?', in Coker (Ed.), *Shifting into Neutral?*, p. 12.

111. Stuart Corbridge, 'Maximising Entropy? New Geographical Orders and the Internationalisation of Business', in George J. Demko and William B. Wood (Eds.), *Reordering the World*, (Boulder, 1994), pp. 281–300 (294).
112. Thompson, *The Pacific Basin since 1945*, pp. 218–31.
113. *ibid.* p. 230; D. Eleanor Westney, 'U.S. Industrial Culture and the Japanese Competitive Challenge', in Alan D. Rosenberg and Tadoshi Yamamoto (Eds.), *Same Bed, Different Dreams: America and Japan – Societies in Transition*, (New York, 1990), pp. 67–82; see Kan Ito, 'Trans-Pacific Anger', *Foreign Policy* 78, (1990), p. 132.
114. A fact bizarrely seized upon by the US ultra-nationalists as suggestive of British recolonisation! Jill Smolowe, 'Enemies of the State', *Time*, 8 May 1995, pp. 22–31 (p. 30).
115. On NAFTA, see, Gustavo Vega (Ed.), 'Symposium on North American Free Trade', *The World Economy*, 17.1, (1991), especially Introduction, pp. 53–5; Richard Buckley, *NAFTA and GATT*, pp. 1–16; David Leyton-Brown, 'The Political Economy of the North American Free Trade Association', in Richard Stubbs and Geoffrey R. D. Underhill (Eds.), *Political Economy and the Changing Global Order*, (London, 1994), pp. 352–65; Gary Clyde Hufbauer and Jeffrey J. Schott, *NAFTA: An Assessment*, (Washington, 1993).
116. Vega, 'Introduction', p. 54.
117. Peter Morici (Ed.), *Making Free Trade Work: The Canada–U.S. Agreement*, (New York, 1990), and *A New Special Relationship: Free Trade and U.S.–Canada Economic Relations in the 1990s*, (Halifax, 1991); Sidney Weintraub (Ed.), *U.S.–Mexican Integration*, (Boulder, 1991).
118. Vega, 'Introduction', p. 54.
119. See n. 109.
120. On the US West coast and Pacific trade, see *The Economist*, 14 September 1991, pp. 43–44. Note that, at present, it is still strongly involved with the Eastern USA, but economic change is differentially occurring in the West and East (see *The Economist*, 14 September 1991, p. 45).
121. *The Economist*, 4 September 1993, p. 57; Paul Perez, 'Economic Policy', in Peele *et al*, *Developments*, pp. 237–52.
122. Henry Brandon (Ed.), *In Search of a New World Order: The Future of U.S. and European Relations*, (Washington, 1992); *The Economist*, 28 September 1991, pp. 49–50; *The Economist*, 3 April 1993, p. 56; *The Economist*, 1 May 1993, pp. 54, 59; Garnham, 'The United States', pp. 12–17; *The Economist*, 4 September 1993, p. 56: 'worldwide the army will shrink from 14 to ten active divisions by 1999 . . . the air force will go from 28 wings to 20 . . . some SS surface ships and submarines will be cut'. Rachel Neaman (Ed.), *The Military Balance 1995/96*, (Oxford, 1995), pp. 19–23.
123. *The Economist*, 29 October 1994, pp. 73.
124. *ibid.*
125. *The Economist*, 25 March 1995, pp. 65–6.
126. *ibid.*
127. According to a recent survey reported in *The Economist*, 22 April 1995, one in six New Yorkers already live in 'extreme poverty', p. 54. See Petras and Morley, *Empire or Republic?*, pp. 82–3, 68–70, 88–90.

128. *ibid.*
129. Although, as Corbridge notes in 'Maximising Entropy', the relative prosperity of the majority of US citizens is declining, p. 271.
130. John Agnew, 'Global Hegemony versus National Economy: The United States in the New World Order', in Demko and Wood, *Reordering the World*, pp. 271–2.
131. *The Economist*, 1 May 1993.
132. *ibid.*
133. Petras and Morley, *Empire or Republic?*, pp. 84–7.
134. *The Economist*, 23 March 1995, p. 67; see also pp. 66–7.
135. Cain, 'Developments', pp. 49–52.
136. Agnew, 'Global Hegemony', pp. 269–70.
137. *The Economist*, 27 June 1992, p. 57.
138. *ibid.*
139. *ibid.*
140. The rise of the 'militias' and other ultra-right-wing groups is notable: see *The Economist*, 29 April 1995, pp. 60–61; *Newsweek*, CXXV(18), 1 May 1995, pp. 12–30; *Time*, 8 May 1995, pp. 21–31 for these groups and their appeal, philosophy, level of militarisation and views on the Oklahoma bombing of 19 April 1995.

3 The Rise of Separatism in Canada

1. For earlier discussions of separatism in Canada see: D. Clift, *Quebec and Nationalism in Crisis*, (Montreal, 1982), A. O. Hero and L. Balthazar, *Contemporary Quebec and the United States*, (Boston, 1988), L. Laczko, 'Canada's Pluralism in Comparative Perspective', *Ethnic and Racial Studies* 17.1 (1994), 20–41, M. Pinard and R. Hamilton, 'The Class Bases of the Quebec Independence Movement', *Ethnic and Racial Studies* 7.1 (1984), 19–54, M. Pinard and R. Hamilton, 'The Quebec Independence Movement', in *National Separatism*, edited by C. Williams, (Cardiff, 1982), pp. 203–33. Canadian history since 1945 is surveyed in R. Bothwell *et al.*, *Canada Since 1945*, (Toronto, 1989), and K. McNaught, *The Pelican History of Canada*, (New York, 1985).
2. R. Hamilton and M. Pinfold, 'The Parti Québécois comes to Power: An Analysis of the 1976 Quebec Election', *Canadian Journal of Political Science*, 11, (1978), (pp. 739–775).
3. Robert C. Vipond, 'Constitution-making in Canada: writing a national identity or preparing for national disintegration?' in Vivien Hart and Shannon C. Stimson (Eds.), *Writing a National Identity: Political, economic and cultural perspectives on the written constitution*, (Manchester, 1993), p. 234.
4. Government of Canada, *Report of the Task Force on Canadian Unity (Pepin-Robarts Report)*, (Hull, Que., 1979), p. A34.
5. For an outline of Canadian history see: J. F. Finlay and D. N. Sprague, *The Structure of Canadian History* (3rd Ed., Toronto, 1989); P. J. Cain and A. G. Hopkins, *British Imperialism: Innovation and Expansion 1688–1914*, (London and New York, 1993), pp. 258–273.
6. As a result of increased immigration from Great Britain, by 1838 the anglophone population of Upper Canada was larger than the francophone

population of Lower Canada and, therefore, the dualist arrangement no longer benefited the British.

7. A. Lijphart, *Democracy in Plural Societies,* (London, 1977), p. 8.
8. This is just one of the tensions at the heart of the debate over the European Union's degree of unity and equality; while Germany historically sees federalism as a force for preserving the character of its constituent parts, the United Kingdom, for example, historically has seen federalisation to be a unifying and homogenising process.
9. See, for example, Kenneth McRoberts, 'The Sources of Neo-Nationalism in Quebec' in Michael D. Behiels (Ed.), *Quebec Since 1945,* (Toronto, 1987), and Kenneth McRoberts, *Quebec: Social Change and Political Crisis,* (Toronto, 1980).
10. McRoberts, 'The Sources of Neo-Nationalism', in Behiels, (Ed.), *Quebec Since 1945.*
11. *ibid.*
12. Lijphart, *Democracy in Plural Societies,* p. 119.
13. McRoberts, 'The Sources of Neo-Nationalism in Quebec', in Behiels (Ed.), *Quebec Since 1945.*
14. David Kwavnick, *The Tremblay Report,* (Toronto, 1973), p. 211.
15. *Proceedings of the Special Senate Committee on the Constitution,* 3rd Session, 13th Parliament, 1974–1978, Senate of Canada, Wednesday 20 September 1978.
16. Peter Russell, *Constitutional Odyssey,* (London, 1992), p. 109.
17. Quebec's expectations of the federal government were expressed by the *Parti Québécois* in its 'White Paper' on sovereignty-association. Government of Quebec, *Quebec-Canada: A New Deal,* (Quebec City, 1979).
18. Michael D. Behiels, 'Quebec: Social Transformation and Ideological Renewal, 1940–1976', in Behiels (Ed.), *Quebec Since 1945.*
19. Keith G. Banting and Richard Simeon, 'Introduction: The Politics of Constitutional Change', in Keith G. Banting and Richard Simeon (Eds.), *The Politics of Constitutional Change in Industrial Nations: Redesigning the State,* (London, 1985), p. 8.
20. *ibid.* p. 10.
21. Pierre Trudeau, *A Time for Action: Towards the Renewal of the Canadian Confederation,* (Hull, Que., 1978).
22. Alan Cairns, 'Citizens (Outsiders) and Governments (Insiders) in Constitution Making: The Case of Meech Lake', *Canadian Public Policy,* Special Issue, September 1988, (pp. 124–128).
23. Indeed, it should be noted that the state still maintains an active role in nurturing linguistic nationalism. The 1977 Bill 101 was declared unconstitutional, but the passage of 'Bill 178' in Quebec's National Assembly in December 1988 further restricted the use of English on public signs. It was enforced through use of the previously little used 'Notwithstanding Clause' which allows legislation to be in place for five years before it can be declared unconstitutional.
24. Leonard Mader, Public Affairs Councillor, High Commission of Canada, London, in interview with A. L. Harris, August 1992.
25. Christine Sypnowich, 'Rights, Community and the Charter', *British Journal of Canadian Studies,* 6(1), (1992), (pp. 39–59).

26. Note that some groups gained more rights than others. Women, for example, received protection of equal rights with men, but aboriginal peoples received only the rights given to them in pre-existing treaties (Charter of Rights and Freedoms, Sections 25 and 27).
27. Banting and Simeon (Eds.), *The Politics of Constitutional Change*, p. 8.
28. *ibid.*
29. Michael D. Behiels (Ed.), *The Meech Lake Primer: Conflicting Views of the 1987 Constitutional Accord*, (Ottawa, 1989).
30. Government of Canada, *Royal Commission on Economic Union and Development Prospects for Canada (MacDonald Report)*, (Hull, Que., 1985), 3(8).
31. Albert Breton, 'The Theory of Competitive Federalism', in Garth Stevenson (Ed.), *Federalism in Canada: Selected Readings*, (Toronto, 1989), p. 457.
32. Cairns, 'Citizens (Outsiders) and Governments (Insiders)', *Canadian Public Policy*, p. S132.
33. *ibid.* p. S125. The fact that they were all white men added to the alienation experienced by women and minority groups.
34. *ibid.* p. S134.
35. *ibid.* p. S135.
36. To be constitutionally enshrined, the Meech Lake Accord had to be unanimously ratified amongst the provinces. By July 1990 it was still unratified in Newfoundland (after its new government withdrew consent) and in Manitoba, where, after a long-drawn-out debate, the vote was irretrievably delayed. Ged Martin, 'Constitution and national identity in contemporary Canada: a historian's view', in Hart and Stimson (Eds.), *Writing a National Identity*, p. 201.
37. Louis Balthazer, *Quebec: A Distinct Society within a Dynamic Canada*, (London, 1989), p. 3.
38. Tony Penikett, 'Constitutionalizing Northern Canada's Colonial Status', in Behiels (Ed.), *The Meech Lake Primer*, pp. 457–464 (p. 458).
39. Cairns, 'Citizens (Outsiders) and Governments (Insiders), *Canadian Public Policy*, p. S134.
40. *ibid.* p. S137.
41. Peter M. Leslie, 'In Defence of the "Spirit of Meech Lake": Evaluating the Criticisms', in Behiels (Ed.), *The Meech Lake Primer*, pp. 483–505 (p. 486).
42. *ibid.* p. 198.
43. Government of Canada, *The History of Canada's Constitutional Development*, (Hull, Que., 1991), p. 15.
44. Russell, *Constitutional Odyssey*, p. 157.
45. *ibid.*
46. Government of Quebec, *Report of the Commission on the Political and Constitutional Future of Quebec (Bélanger-Campeau Report)*, (Quebec City, 1991), p. 72.
47. Russell, *Constitutional Odyssey*, p. 166.
48. *Macleans*, 4 May 1992, p. 3.
49. *Macleans*, 6 January 1992, p. 19.
50. Government of Canada, *The Charlottetown Consensus 1992*, (Hull, Que., 1992).

51. The 'Yes' campaign was also backed by the Royal Bank of Canada, which, in an influential report claimed that over two million new jobs would be created as a result of a 'Yes' vote, whereas over one million Canadians would emigrate if there was a 'No' vote. *The Economist*, 3 October 1992, pp. 68–69. See also Royal Bank of Canada, *Unity or Disunity: The Benefits and the Costs*, (Montreal, 1992).

52. *Globe and Mail*, 20 August 1992.

53. *ibid.*

54. Annis May Timpson, 'To be or not to be: a sovereign Quebec?', *The World Today*, 50(11), (1994), (pp. 202–203), p. 202.

55. *ibid.*

56. *The Economist*, 10 December 1994, p. 71.

57. *ibid.*

58. Secrétariat de la Commission, *Mastering our Future: Policy Programme of the Quebec Liberal Party*, (Quebec City, 1985), p. 100.

59. Government of Quebec, *Partners for a Skilled and Competitive Quebec: Policy Statement on Labour Force Development*, (Quebec City, 1991), p. 61.

60. *ibid.* pp. 47–59.

61. In 1991 only 4.4 per cent of immigrants to Quebec were from France, compared to 50.1 per cent from the Asian continent and 12.3 per cent from the African continent. While a steadily increasing number of immigrants come from these continents, the number of European immigrants is declining rapidly. Government of Quebec, *Immigration Statistics*, (Quebec City, 1992).

62. Government of Quebec, *Report of the Commission on the Political and Constitutional Future of Quebec*, p. 10.

63. Government of Canada, *Report of the Task Force on Canadian Unity*, (Hull, Que., 1979), p. 10.

64. In the 1993 election the Conservatives lost all but two of their 170 seats, while the Liberals formed a majority with 177 of the 295 seats. The *Bloc Québécois* formed the Official Opposition, while the Reform Party swept the West, taking 52 seats.

65. *The Economist*, 30 October 1993, p. 67.

66. In February 1994, in response to a Reform Party poll, 79 per cent of Westerners indicated that they would prefer the right to recall an MP who was not found to be satisfactory. *The Economist*, 26 March 1994, p. 82.

67. Charles, 'Quebec and the Future of Canada', Lecture given at Robinson College, Cambridge, UK, 21 May 1992.

68. Roger Gibbons, 'Barometer Falling: the Canadian Constitutional Environment', *British Journal of Canadian Studies*, 6(1), (1991), (pp. 8–17), p. 12.

4   The Legacy of State-Formation in the Contemporary Politics of the Americas

1. On 'political cultures' see, for example, R. Bollington, *Culture and Society*, (London, 1991), D. J. Elkins and R. E. B. Simeon, 'A Cause in

Search of Its Effect or What Does Political Culture Explain?', *Comparative Politics* 13 (1979), 127–45, R. Inglehart, *Changing Culture*, (Princeton, 1989).

2. See for example, Robert L. Devaney, *An Introduction to Chaotic Dynamical Systems,* (Menlo Park, 1978); Theodor Schwenk, *Sensitive Chaos*, (New York, 1976); James Gleik, *Chaos, Making a New Science,* (New York, 1987); Ian Stewart, *The Problems of Mathematics,* (Oxford, 1987).

3. The following account of Argentina's and Peru's history is based on Thomas E. Skidmore and Peter H. Smith, *Modern Latin America*, (3rd Ed., New York, 1992), pp. 68–111 and 185–220. See also, Mark A. Burkholder and Lyman L. Johnson, *Colonial Latin America*, (2nd Ed., Cambridge, 1994), pp. 305–6, and especially 310–12. For the broader political and cultural context of Latin American history, and the present international politics of Latin America, see: G. Pope Atkins, *Latin America in the International Political System*, (Boulder, 1994), Leslie Bethel (Ed.), *The Cambridge History of Latin America*, (Cambridge, 1995), Leslie Bethel (Ed.), *Ideas and Ideologies in Latin America since 1870*, (Cambridge, 1995), Peter Calvert, *The International Politics of Latin America*, (Manchester, 1994), Howard J. Wiarda and Harvey F. Kline (Ed.), *Latin American Politics and Development*, (Boulder, 1994).

4. This account is based on Skidmore and Smith, *Modern Latin America,* pp. 221–53. See also, Burkholder and Johnson, *Colonial,* pp. 320–4.

5. For general surveys of colonial and early independent American history see Maldwyn A. Jones, *The Limits of Liberty* (2nd Ed., Oxford, 1995), pp. 1–112, Richard Middleton, *Colonial America: a History, 1607–1760*, (Oxford, 1992). The following account is based on these and other works cited in endnotes.

6. Hugh Brogan, *The Pelican History of the United States of America,* (London, 1987), p. 22.

7. *ibid.* pp. 10–11.

8. *ibid.* p. 13.

9. *ibid.* p. 15.

10. *ibid.* p. 24.

11. Carl N. Degler, *Out of Our Past: The Forces that Shaped Modern America,* (3rd Ed., London, 1984), p. 26.

12. *ibid.* p. 3.

13. George B. Tindall and David E. Shi, *America: A Narrative History,* (2nd Ed., London, 1989), p. 20.

14. Brogan, *The Pelican History of the United States,* p. 39.

15. *ibid.* p. 44.

16. *ibid.* p. 45.

17. Degler, *Out of Our Past,* p. 5.

18. *ibid.* p. 27.

19. Jones, *The Limits of Liberty,* p. 10.

20. Brogan, *The Pelican History of the United States,* p. 48.

21. Jones, *The Limits of Liberty,* p. 10.

22. *ibid.* p. 11.

23. *ibid.*

24. *ibid.* p. 12.

25. *ibid.* p. 13.
26. Middleton, *Colonial America*, p. 188.
27. *ibid.* p. 186.
28. Phillip D. Morgan (Ed.), *Diversity and Unity in Early North America*, (London, 1993), p. xi.
29. Jack P. Greene, 'Convergence: Development of an American Society, 1720–1780', in Morgan (Ed.), *Diversity and Unity*, pp. 43–72 (p. 46).
30. *ibid.* p. 47.
31. Ira Berlin, 'Time, Space and the Evolution of Afro-American Society on Mainland British America', in Morgan (Ed.), *Diversity and Unity*, pp. 113–146 (p. 116).
32. *ibid.*
33. *ibid.* p. 125.
34. *ibid.* p. 128.
35. Jack P. Greene, 'Convergence: Development of an American Society, 1720–1780', in Morgan (Ed.), *Diversity and Unity*, p. 44.
36. Bernard Bailyn, 'A Domesday Book for the Periphery', in Morgan (Ed.), *Diversity and Unity*, pp. 11–42 (p. 14).
37. Greene, 'Convergence: Development of an American Society, 1720–1780', p. 50.
38. *ibid.* p. 54.
39. *ibid.* p. 55.
40. John M. Murrin, 'Beneficiaries of Catastrophe: the English Colonists in America', in Morgan (Ed.), *Diversity and Unity*, pp. 259–282 (p. 270).
41. Bailyn, 'A Domesday Book for the Periphery', p. 15.
42. Middleton, *Colonial America*, p. 153.
43. Bailyn, 'A Domesday Book for the Periphery', p. 31.
44. Murrin, 'Beneficiaries of Catastrophe: the English Colonists in America', p. 273.
45. Bailyn, 'A Domesday Book for the Periphery', p. 24.
46. *ibid.* p. 28.
47. *ibid.* p. 35.
48. Greene, 'Convergence: Development of an American Society, 1720–1780', p. 61.
49. Jonathan C. D. Clark, *The Language of Liberty 1660–1832: Political Discourse and Social Dynamics in the Anglo-American World*, (Cambridge, 1994), p. 13.
50. *ibid.* p. 9.
51. John Agnew, 'The United States and American Hegemony', in *Political Geography of the Twentieth Century*, edited by Peter J. Taylor, (London, 1993), pp. 207–238 (pp. 211–212).
52. Arthur M. Schlesinger, *The Cycles of American History*, (Boston, 1988), p. 137.
53. Agnew, 'The United States', pp. 211–212.

5 The Global Context of American Instability

1. Kennedy's 'great powers' are more than our near-equal players in multipolar global politics, but what others might describe as regional hegemons or even 'superpowers'.
2. M. Hogan (Ed.), *The End of the Cold War*, (New York, 1992); John L. Gaddis, *The United States and the End of the Cold War*, (New York, 1992); Charles Krauthammer, 'The Unipolar Moment', *Foreign Affairs*, 70(1), (1991), 23–33; Christopher Layne, 'The Unipolar Illusion: Why New Great Powers will Rise', *International Security*, 17, (1993), 5–51.
3. Michael Kidron and Ronald Segal, *The New State of the World Atlas*, (4th Ed., London, 1991), pp. 76–7 and 146; Anthony Smith, *The Geopolitics of Information*, (London, 1980).
4. Francis Fukuyama, *The End of History and the Last Man*, (New York, 1992).
5. Charles W. Kegley, Jr., 'The New Global Order: The power of principle in a pluralistic world', *Ethics and International Affairs*, 6, (1992), 21–40. For responses see, Robert Jervis, 'Will the New World be Better?', in Robert Jervis and Seweryn Bialer (Eds.), *Soviet-American Relations after the Cold War*, (Durham, N.C., 1991), pp. 7–19; Michael Cox, 'The New World Order', *Politics Review*, 2.4, (1993), pp. 7–9, 'Whatever Happened to the "New World Order"?', *Critique*, 25, (1993), 95–107, and 'Rethinking the End of the Cold War', *Review of International Studies*, 20, (1994), pp. 187–200 and references (especially those cited in note 20, p. 190).
6. James Petras and Morris Morley, *Empire or Republic? American Global Power and Domestic Decay*, (London, 1995), pp. 131–2; L. Freedman and E. Karsh, *The Gulf Conflict 1990–91*, (London, 1993); D. McDowall, *The Kurds*, (London, 1991); J. Zametica, *The Yugoslav Crisis*, (London, 1992).
7. Gabriella Graselli, 'The Anglo-American Relationship in the Twenty-first century', *The Oxford International Review*, V.2, (1994), 15–18.
8. *Americas Review 1993/4*, (13th Ed., 1994), pp. 153–66 (p. 153).
9. Steffan Schmidt *et al.*, *American Government and Politics Today 1995–1996 Edition*, (St Paul, 1995), pp. XLVII–XLIX.
10. Carl W. Kester, *Japanese Takeovers: the Global Contest for Corporate Control*, (Cambridge, Mass., 1991); Denis Encarnation, *Rivals Beyond Trade: America versus Japan in Global Competition*, (Ithaca, 1992).
11. Notably, of course, Paul Kennedy, *The Rise and Fall of the Great Powers*, (London, 1987), esp. pp. 591–608.
12. Rachel Neaman (Ed.), *The Military Balance 1994–1995*, (London, 1994), pp. 13–14.
13. *ibid.*, pp. 13–33.
14. K. R. Dark, 'Europe, NATO and the End of the Cold War', in *New Studies in Post-Cold War Security*, edited by K. R. Dark, (Aldershot, 1996).
15. Zbigniew Brzezinski, *Out of Control: Global Turmoil on the Eve of the 21st Century*, (New York, 1993), esp. pp. 167–81. Note that this may be accompanied by a decline in US hegemony in cultural affairs elsewhere: William E. Schmidt, 'In Europe, America's Grip on Pop Culture is Fading', *New York Times*, 23 March 1993.
16. Fergus Carr, *NATO and the New European Security*, (London, 1994);

Paul R. S. Gebhard, *The United States and European Security*, (London, 1994); Mathias Jopp, *The Strategic Implications of European Integration*, (London, 1994).

17. On Bretton Woods and its effects: Eric Helleiner, 'From Bretton Woods to Global Finance: A World Turned Upside Down', in Richard Stubbs and Geoffrey R. D. Underhill (Eds.), *Political Economy and the Changing Global Order*, (Basingstoke, 1994), pp. 163–75.

18. Charles W. Kegley, Jr. and Eugene R. Witkopf, *World Politics: Trend and Transformation*, (4th Ed., New York, 1993), p. 430.

19. *ibid.*

20. *ibid.*

21. *ibid.*, and p. 431.

22. *ibid.*; Neaman, *The Military Balance*, p. 13.

23. On the war and misperceptions see, L. Freedman and E. Karsh, *The Gulf Conflict 1990–1991*, (London, 1993); R. Dannreuther, *The Gulf Conflict*, (London, 1993); Fred Halliday, 'The Gulf War 1990–1991 and the study of International Relations', *Review of International Studies*, 20.2, (1994), 109–30; E. Bresheeth and N. Yuval-Davis, *The Gulf War and the New World Order*, (London, 1991); Jeffrey McCausland, *The Gulf Conflict: a Military Analysis*, (London, 1993).

24. Charles W. Kegley, 'How did the Cold War Die? Principles for an Autopsy', *Mershon International Studies Review*, 38 (Supplement 1), (1993), (pp. 11–41).

25. Neaman, *The Military Balance*, pp. 13–14.

26. L. Dunn, *Containing Nuclear Proliferation*, (London, 1991), pp. 258–61; B. Roberts, *Chemical Disarmament and International Security*, (London, 1992); V. Utgoff, *The Challenge of Chemical Weapons*, (London, 1990); B. Buch and C. Flowers, *International Handbook on Chemical Weapons Proliferation*, (New York, 1991).

27. Neaman, *The Military Balance*, pp. 260–1.

28. C. Bluth, *Inaugural Lecture*, Graduate School of European and International Studies, University of Reading, 1995.

29. Note the psychological effects of the Oklahoma bombing as reported by, *Newsweek*, 1 May 1995, CXXV(18), pp. 11–20; *Time*, 1 May 1995, 145(17), p. 46.

30. For two recent reviews of this question see, R. J. Barry Jones, *Globalisation and Interdependence in the International Political Economy*, (London, 1995); James Rosenau and Ernst-Otto Czempiel (Eds.), *Governance without Government: Order and Change in World Politics*, (Cambridge, 1992). For an overview of the academic literature see, Paul R. Viotti and Mark V. Kauppi, *International Relations Theory*, (New York, 1993), pp. 228–448.

31. Philip Cerny, 'Gridlock and Decline: Financial Internationalization, Banking Politics and the American Political Process', in Stubbs and Underhill, *Political Economy*, pp. 425–38; Philip Cerny, *Finance and World Politics: Models, Regimes and States in the post-Hegemonic Era*, (Cheltenham, 1993); Richard Maidment and James Thurber (Eds.), *The Politics of Relative Decline*, (Oxford and New York, 1993).

32. Robert Gilpin, *The Political Economy of International Relations*, (Princeton, 1987), p. 332.

33. On Europe: Samuel P. Huntington, 'The US – Decline or Renewal?', *Foreign Affairs*, 67, (1988/89), pp. 84–8. On Germany: Jeffrey E. Garten, *A Cold Peace: America, Japan, Germany and the Struggle for Supremacy*, (New York, 1992). For an interesting analysis of the prospect of an EU 'superpower', see, Jacques Attali, *Lignes d'Horizon*, (Paris, 1990).
34. On the 'New European Security Order' see, Barry Buzan *et al.* (Eds.), *The European Security Order Recast*, (London, 1990); R. Ullman, *Securing Europe*, (Princeton, 1991); A. Hyde-Price, *European Security Beyond the Cold War*, (London, 1991).
35. Dark, 'Europe, NATO and the End of the Cold War'.
36. Carr, *NATO;* Gebhard, *The United States.*
37. David Garnham, 'The United States in Decline?', in Christopher Coker (Ed.), *Shifting into Neutral?*, (London, 1990), pp. 3–21 (p. 15).
38. For a dissident voice, Charles W. Kegley and Gregory Raymond, *A Multipolar Peace? Great-Power Politics in the Twenty-first Century*, (New York, 1994), p. 25.
39. See n. 34
40. Christopher Coker, 'Intimations of Mortality?', in Coker (Ed.), *Shifting into Neutral?*, pp. 22–40 (25).
41. Garnham, 'The United States in Decline?', in Coker (Ed.), *Shifting into Neutral?*, pp. 13 and 15.
42. Garten, *A Cold Peace.*
43. Britain fought in the Falklands: P. Calvert, *The Falklands*, (London, 1982); L. Freedman and V. Gamba-Stonehouse, *Signals of War*, (London, 1990); J. Gobel, *The Struggle for the Falkland Islands*, (Newhaven, 1982); W. Smith, *Towards Resolution*, (Boulder, 1991). France intervened in Chad and (in the 1990s) Rwanda; on Chad see, J. Wright, *Libya, Chad and the Central Sahara*, (New York, 1989).
44. Dark, 'Europe, NATO and the End of the Cold War'.
45. Neaman (Ed.), *The Military Balance*, passim.
46. Dark, 'Europe, NATO and the End of the Cold War'.
47. Paul Kennedy, *Preparing for the Twenty-first Century*, (London, 1994).
48. *ibid.*
49. Kennedy, *The Rise and Fall of the Great Powers*. See also, Robert B. Oxnam, 'Asia/Pacific Challenges', *Foreign Affairs*, 72(1) (1992/3), 58–73.
50. Roger C. Thompson, *The Pacific Basin since 1945*, (Harlow, 1994), pp. 4–10; Gerald Segal, *Rethinking the Pacific*, (Oxford, 1990), pp. 83, 100–1; Richard B. Finn, *Winners in Peace: MacArthur, Yoshida and Postwar Japan*, (Berkeley, 1992).
51. Thompson, *The Pacific Basin*, p. 12.
52. Geir Lundestad, *East, West, North, South*, trans. Gail Adams Kvam, (2nd Ed., Oslo, 1991), p. 219.
53. Thompson, *The Pacific Basin*, p. 7.
54. Lundestad, *East, West, North, South*, pp. 219–21.
55. Segal, *Rethinking the Pacific*, p. 297.
56. Lundestad, *East, West, North, South*, pp. 221.
57. Segal, *Rethinking the Pacific*, pp. 299–302; Colin Mackerras, Pradeep Taneja and Graham Young, *China since 1978*, (New York, 1993), pp. 232–4 and 214–19.

58. Discussed in Joseph S. Nye, *Bound to Lead*, (New York, 1990), pp. 154–5. See also, Paul Krugman, *The Age of Diminished Expectations: US Economic Policy in the 1990s*, (Cambridge, Mass., 1990).

59. Takashi Inoguchi, *Japan's International Relations*, (London, 1991), pp. 9–37.

60. Garnham, 'The United States in Decline?', in Coker (Ed.), *Shifting into Neutral?*, p. 12.

61. *ibid.*

62. Peter J. Katzenstein and Nobuo Okawara, 'Japan's National Security: Structures, Norms and Policies', *International Security*, 17, (1993), pp. 84–118.

63. Susan Strange, *States and Markets: An Introduction to International Political Economy*, (London, 1988), p. 133. On the paucity of Japanese religious 'exports', for instance, see, Joanne O'Brien and Martin Palmer, *The State of Religion Atlas*, (London, 1993), pp. 21, 35.

64. Inoguchi, *Japan's International Relations*; K. V. Kesavan (Ed.), *Contemporary Japanese Politics and Foreign Policy*, (New Delhi, 1989); Gerald Curtis (Ed.), *Japan's Foreign Policy after the Cold War*, (Armonk, 1993).

65. This is not to say that the Japanese government does not seek a greater regional role: Hisane Masaki, 'Japan Adopts a New Asia Policy', *The Japan Times Weekly*, International edition, 11–17 January 1993, pp. 1, 6; Nye, *Bound to Lead*, p. 169.

66. For discussions of Japan's role in the Pacific and global economy, and its prospects in the near future see, Gavin Boyd, *Pacific Trade, Investment and Politics*, (London, 1989); Janos Radvanji (Ed.), *The Pacific in the 1990s: Economic and Strategic Change*, (Lanham, 1990); Bill Emmott, *The Sun Also Sets: the Limits to Japan's Economic Power* (New York, 1991); Bella Balassa and Marcus Noland, *Japan in the World Economy*, (Washington, 1988).

67. For a discussion of the 'fragility' of the East Asian economies see, Hamish McRae, *The World in 2020*, (London, 1995), pp. 70–93.

68. For an introduction to the recent history of China and its role in the Pacific region, see, Edwin E. Moise, *Modern China: A History*, (2nd Ed., London, 1994); Mackerras, Taneja and Young, *China Since 1978*, esp. p. 241; John King Fairbank, *China: A New History*, (Cambridge, Mass., 1992).

69. Gregory C. Chow, *The Chinese Economy*, (New York, 1985); Carl Riskin, *China's Political Economy: The Quest for Development since 1949*, (Oxford, 1987).

70. Neaman, *The Military Balance*, pp. 170–3.

71. Gordon White, *Riding the Tiger: the Politics of Economic Reform in post-Mao China*, (London, 1993); Lucien W. Pye, 'China: A Superpower?', *The Oxford International Review*, VI(1), (1994), 18–25.

72. Moise, *Modern China*, pp. 216–225.

73. *ibid.* pp. 223–5; Judith Bannister, *China's Changing Population*, (Stanford, 1987); Elisabeth Croll *et al.* (Eds.), *China's one-Child Family Policy*, (London, 1985).

74. Harry Harding, *A Fragile Relationship: Sino-American Relations since 1972*, (Washington, 1992).

75. Rosemary Foot, 'Neither Friends nor Enemies: Sino-American Relations after the Cold War', *Oxford International Review,* V. 2, (1994), 19–22; Moise, *Modern China,* pp. 202–3.
76. Anita Chan, 'The Challenge to the Social Fabric', in David Goodman and Gerald Segal, *China at Forty: Mid-Life Crisis?,* (Oxford, 1989), pp. 66–85.
77. Merle Goldman, 'Dissent in China after 1989', *The Oxford International Review,* VI(1), (1994), pp. 26–7 and 57; Geremie Barme, 'Notes on Chinese Culture in the 1990s', *Current History,* (1994), pp. 270–75.
78. Chan, 'The Challenge'; Mackerras, Taneja and Young, *China since 1978,* pp. 170–1 and 178.
79. Timothy Brook, *Quelling the People: The Military Suppression of the Beijing Democracy Movement,* (Oxford, 1992); Andrew Nathan, *China's Crisis,* (New York, 1990); Lee Feigon, *China Rising: The Meaning of Tiananmen,* (Chicago, 1990).
80. Mackerras, Taneja and Young, *China Since 1978,* pp. 41–2; Moise, *Modern China,* pp. 225–8.
81. Clarke D. Neher, *Southeast Asia in the New International Era,* (2nd Ed., Boulder, 1994).
82. G. Arnold, *South Africa,* (London, 1992); R. Oliver, *The African Experience,* (New York, 1992).
83. Raymond Takeyh and John L. Esposito, 'The Islamic Threat: Myth or Reality?', *The Oxford International Review,* VI(1), (1994), pp. 58–9; J. Harbeson and D. Rothschild, *Africa in World Politics,* (Boulder, 1991).
84. Segal, *Rethinking the Pacific,* pp. 252–3; Thompson, *The Pacific Basin,* pp. 286–7, 348–51.
85. Note that others of these states may soon join the Security Council: Paul Lewis, 'US Backs Council Seats for Bonn and Tokyo', *The New York Times,* 29 January 1993, p. 16.
86. 'Wars of the 21st Century' (interview with Martin van Creveld), *Newsweek,* CXXV(16), 17 April 1995, p. 54.

Index

aboriginal peoples, 45, 53–4, 62, 72, 73, 74, 80, 82, 83, 84, 85, 88, 89, 92, 96, 121
absolutism, 59
Acapulco Commitment for Peace, Development and Democracy, 24
Adams, John Quincy, 47
African-Americans, 44–6, 48–9, 63, 64, 70
agriculture, 55, 56, 113, 114, 116
Alamo, 43
Alaska, 8, 13, 43, 54, 62, 70, 145
Alberta, 56
'Alliance for Progress', 23
'Americanisation', 131; see also culture
anti-Americanism, 3, 128–9
Arbenz, Jacobo, 23
Argentina, 101–3, 104
Arizona, 43, 59
Arkansas, 45
Asia–Pacific region, 13–14, 17, 26, 63, 64, 66, 67, 137–42
Australasia, 69, 142
Australia, see Australasia
authoritarianism, 145

Balkans, 8
Barbados, 113, 115, 120
Beaudoin-Edwards Committee, 89
behaviouralism, 100
Belgium, 27
biculturalism, 78, 79
bilingualism, 78, 79, 88
Bill 101, see under Quebec
Bill of Rights (US), 53
bipolarity, 29
Black Nationalism, 45–6, 51
Bloc Québécois, see under Quebec
Bosnia, 61, 130, 131
Bourassa, Robert, 84, 91
Brazil, 17, 23, 65, 119, 123

Bretton Woods, 18, 65, 131
British Columbia, 13
British North America, 12–13, 115, 121, 123
British North America Act, 20, 53, 72, 76, 82, 83, 88
Bush, George, 20, 27, 36, 43, 130, 131
'butterfly effect', see 'extreme sensitivity'

California, 42–4, 59, 64, 65, 145
Canada, 2, 12–13, 20–1, 24–5, 40–1, 42, 46, 50–5, 56–8, 64, 66, 67, 70, 72–97, 144
canadiens, see under Quebec
capitalism, 4, 18, 138, 140
Carolinas, 12, 113, 114, 116, 117
Castro, Fidel, 59
Central Asia, 28, 141
Charles II, 111
Charlottetown Agreement, see Charlottetown Consensus
Charlottetown Conference (1865), 85
Charlottetown Consensus (1992), 54, 73, 89, 90–2, 95
Charter of Rights and Freedoms, 51, 53, 74, 81–2, 83, 84, 85, 88, 95, 96
Chile, 20
China, 14, 27–9, 36, 38, 48, 129, 138, 139–42
Chrétien, Jean, 95
'Citizen's Forum on Canada's Future', 89, 90
Civil Rights Movement, 45, 47, 48
Civil War (American), 44, 47
class, 25, 50, 77, 102, 106, 112, 118, 144
Cleveland, Grover, 14
Clinton, Bill, 58, 130
Cold War, 1, 2, 3, 8, 9, 10, 17, 18,

169